Ernest Gaines

Twayne's United States Authors Series

Frank Day, Editor

Clemson University

TUSAS 584

ERNEST GAINES
Photograph courtesy of JCA, New York.

Ernest Gaines

Valerie Melissa Babb

Georgetown University

Twayne Publishers
A Division of G. K. Hall & Co. • Boston

Ernest Gaines
Valerie Melissa Babb

Copyright 1991 by G. K. Hall & Co.
All rights reserved.
Published by Twayne Publishers
A division of G. K. Hall & Co.
70 Lincoln Street
Boston, Massachusetts 02111

Copyediting supervised by Barbara Sutton.
Book production by Gabrielle B. McDonald.
Typeset in Garamond by Graphic Sciences Corporation, Cedar Rapids, Iowa.

First published 1991.
10 9 8 7 6 5 4 3 2 1

Library of Congress Cataloging-in-Publication Data

Babb, Valerie Melissa.
    Ernest Gaines / Valerie Melissa Babb.
        p.   cm. — (Twayne's United States authors series ; TUSAS 584)
    Includes bibliographical references and index.
    ISBN 0-8057-7630-3 (alk. paper)
    1. Gaines, Ernest J., 1933-   —Criticism and interpretation.
    I. Title.   II. Series.
    PS3557.A355Z59   1991
    813'.54—dc20   91-2968

To Jaren, as I look to the future;
to Dorothy Lorraine and Handel McCartney Babb,
as I look to the past

Contents

Preface

In 1971 *The Autobiography of Miss Jane Pittman* established Ernest J. Gaines as a major American writer. This landmark story, later made into a television movie, captured the attention of a nation increasingly preoccupied with new insights into its slavery, Civil War, and civil rights epochs. Miss Jane became a national treasure, continuing the chronicle of Margaret Walker's *Jubilee* (1967) and anticipating the saga of Alex Haley's *Roots* (1976).

The delicate intertwining of history with an individual's quiet quest for human dignity gives Jane's story the enduring, universal appeal that marks all Gaines's fiction. His texts are peopled with characters every reader feels intimately acquainted with, characters whose cadences realistically render the mysticism, traditions, and legends of the rural Louisiana experience that inspires his fiction. Creating narrators based on the storytellers he heard in his youth, Gaines details accounts of love and hate, change and resistance to change, personal discovery and personal development. The fictional environs of Bayonne, a locale that, like Faulkner's Yoknapatawpha, acts as a setting for all Gaines's writing, is a landscape of decaying plantations, tenant farms, and bayous rendered with such undeniable authenticity that readers feel they have been privy to a vanishing milieu.

Like *Miss Jane*, all Gaines's novels—*Catherine Carmier, Of Love and Dust, In My Father's House,* and *A Gathering of Old Men*—as well as his collection of short stories, *Bloodline,* blend experience native to Louisiana with universal human conditions. It is precisely this balance between the specific and the universal that gives his written work such wide appeal to both general and more specialized audiences. Television adaptations of *The Autobiography of Miss Jane Pittman* and *A Gathering of Old Men* met with enthusiastic popular response, and the quality of Gaines's fiction has earned consistent professional recognition. He has been the recipient of many awards, among them the Joseph Henry Jackson Literary Award in 1959, a National Endowment for the Arts grant in 1966, and a Guggenheim Fellowship in 1974. He has also received an honorary doctorate from Denison University and a visiting professorship in creative writing from the University of Southwestern Louisiana, Lafayette.

By reviewing Gaines's work in chronological sequence, this study identifies his trademarks: the mining of Louisiana's rich cultural reserve and the use of communal narrative to replicate in writing the oral storytelling intrinsic to his native area. The first chapter details those aspects of his life and career which inspire the recurrent strains in his literature. Chapter 2 addresses the manner in which he draws on the universal theme of the quest, to illuminate the importance of personal dignity. Chapter 3 charts Gaines's growing use of the pastoral in his treatment of individual nihilism. The fourth chapter probes his tragic vision of the individual unsuccessfully battling the laws of society, and the fifth examines his use of a fictitious autobiography as a revisionist sociocultural epic. In chapters 6 and 7 his interpretation of leadership and protest in black culture is investigated, and the final chapter attempts to illuminate Gaines's contribution to American letters. Even though this study takes a chronological approach to his writing, an exception is made in discussing *Bloodline* prior to discussing the novels. Though *Catherine Carmier* and *Of Love and Dust* were his first two published, full-length works, some of the stories in *Bloodline* predate them, and the short stories provide an exemplary framework for understanding the rest of Gaines's canon.

For clarity, each chapter addresses a separate work, but it should be noted that the particular aspects accentuated exist to varying degrees in all works. Several texts share participatory narrators who assist in developing stories as well as telling them; others have in common themes treating the legacy of slavery, the quest for black manhood, and the importance of remembering the past; still others share the motifs of change and stasis, individual and communal displacement. Though his literature is always universal, the use of folk forms also makes it particular to black Louisiana experience. In all texts, key elements of black culture—the blues, sermons, oral histories, the black preacher, hoodoo priestesses, spirituals, and black mythology—recur and firmly root his works in an African-American tradition.

Taken as a whole, Gaines's canon represents a blending of Louisiana, African-American, and universal human experience. His writings reproduce the communal nature of storytelling in his rural parish while accenting the historicity that joins members of the African-American diaspora to larger American society. By recording and preserving his people's culture in his literature, Gaines creates both an ongoing memorial to a vanishing way of life and an enduring testament to eternal human concerns.

Acknowledgments

My thanks to Dr. William C. Fischer, professor of English at the State University of New York at Buffalo, for the guidance that nurtured my interest in literary representations of African-American oral culture.

I am also grateful to my family, friends, and colleagues for their support in the writing of this work, and in particular to Hyacinth Loney, without whose help and generous donation of her time this book would never have been realized, and to her sister Hazel Loney.

For permission to quote from copyrighted material, acknowledgment is made to the following: Alfred Knopf, Inc., for *A Gathering of Old Men* (1983) and *In My Father's House* (1978); Doubleday, Inc., for *Bloodline* (1968) and *The Autobiography of Miss Jane Pittman* (1971); Northpoint Press for *Catherine Carmier* (1964, 1981); and Ernest J. Gaines and the JCA Literary Agency for *Of Love and Dust* (1979) and "Miss Jane and I" (1978).

Chronology

1933   Ernest J. Gaines born, 15 January, in Point Coupée Parish, Oscar, Louisiana, the first child of Manuel and Adrienne J. (Colar) Gaines.

1948   Moves to Vallejo, California, to join his parents and continue his schooling.

1956   First short story, "The Turtles," published in *Transfer* magazine.

1957   Graduates from San Francisco State College and is awarded the Wallace Stegner Creative Writing Fellowship.

1958   Begins study at Stanford University. Greatly encouraged by Malcolm Cowley. Publishes story "A Long Day in November."

1959   Receives the Joseph Henry Jackson Literary Award for the short story "Comeback."

1962   Story "Just Like a Tree."

1963   Story "The Sky Is Gray."

1964   *Catherine Carmier* (novel).

1966   Receives National Endowment for the Arts grant.

1967   *Of Love and Dust* (novel).

1968   *Bloodline* (collection of short stories).

1971   "A Long Day in November" (taken from the *Bloodline* collection) is published separately as a children's book. Writer-in-residence, Denison University, Granville, Ohio. *The Autobiography of Miss Jane Pittman* (novel).

1972   Receives the Louisiana Library Award; the California Gold Medal for the best book by a Californian for the year; and the Black Academy of Arts and Letters Fiction Award.

1974   Receives a Guggenheim Fellowship. *The Autobiography of Miss Jane Pittman* airs as a television movie.

1978   *In My Father's House* (novel).

1980   Is awarded honorary doctorate of literature from Denison University.

1983   A *Gathering of Old Men* (novel). Visiting professor, University of Southwestern Louisiana, Lafayette.

1984   A *Gathering of Old Men* airs as television movie.

Chapter One
The Bayou *Griot*

The term *griot* has been used variously to refer to oral historians, poets, and singers. Its West African origins have been traced to both the Fulani and the Wolof languages, and in both it has described those who sing praises, recite genealogies, and pass on histories.[1] Through the *griot* the poems, music, current events, and lore of particular communities were dispersed over wide areas. The term is instructive in understanding the work of Ernest Gaines and his uniqueness as a writer. In a fundamental sense he is a *griot* of the bayous, plantations, and former slave quarters that form the Pointe Coupée Parish of his youth. His literature vivifies the history, local events, and mix of African-American, Cajun, and Creole heritages that compose the multi-cultural identity of this cloistered community. Gathering communal lore, he secures the perpetuity of Pointe Coupée by passing on its character to a larger literary audience.[2]

The oldest boy of Manuel and Adrienne Colar Gaines's nine boys and three girls was born on 15 January 1933. His birthplace was the River Lake Plantation in Pointe Coupée Parish, Louisiana, a locale whose flavor and presence were later to fire Gaines's imagination and permeate all his fiction. His father was a laborer on a local plantation, and Gaines himself worked in the fields near Baton Rouge, Louisiana. His parents separated when he was very young, and the absence of his father would later contribute in part to the genesis of one of his major themes, sons searching for fathers. Even as a child he attempted artistic creation in the form of writing and directing church plays, but Gaines did not truly discover his appreciation for litera-ture until he absented his Louisiana home.

In 1948, when he was 15, Gaines left the picturesque beauty of rural Louisiana and came to Vallejo, California, with his mother and his step-father, Raphael Norbert Colar, Sr., a merchant seaman. Because there were no adequate schools in his native area of Louisiana, his mother and step-father thought it best that Gaines continue his education in California. When he arrived in Vallejo, he and his parents relocated to a section of gov-ernment housing peopled with children from a mixture of races and cultures—whites, blacks, Chicanos, Filipinos, Japanese, and Chinese. Though he was lonely for home, the racial and ethnic variety of his new surroundings was reminiscent of the cultural mixture that characterized his Louisiana parish, and Gaines was able to adapt to his northern California milieu. When his parents moved out of the projects, however, the tenuous comfort he had developed would be replaced by a feeling of isolation.

In his new neighborhood his potential friends were associations his stepfather did not want Gaines to develop. Accustomed to the rigorous discipline of the merchant marine, Raphael Colar forbade him to dissipate his energies in meaningless activities and dallying on the streets with other teenagers who might prove to be bad influences. As a result Gaines spent much of his time in the Vallejo Public Library, lonely, homesick, and seeking reading material on the very world he had left behind. It was during his solitary hours in the library that his interest in writing was fostered, and he credits his stepfather with incidentally nurturing his nascent absorption in literature. With other social outlets interdicted by Raphael Colar, Gaines turned to books to dispel the growing alienation caused by the divorce from his Louisiana community.

The move to California turned out to be an experience of displacement for the adolescent Gaines. In recalling the difficulty he had in packing, he reveals his reluctance to leave his birthplace and recites the very items that represent Louisiana to him and symbolically bind him to the world of his rural parish: "It took me all day to pack, unpack, and repack the old brown leather suitcase. I didn't have many clothes . . . but for some reason I could not get it done. Maybe it was the bag of oranges, or the shoebox of fried chicken and bread, or the tea cakes and pralines wrapped in brown paper, or the bag of unshelled pecans—maybe it was one of these or all of these that kept me opening and shutting the suitcase."[3] Gaines's vacillation can be attributed to more than a change of locales. As a southerner he was uprooting and subsequently settling in a place with a different history, different traditions, customs, and values. The remembrance of this dislodging would influence much of his fiction, whether through his treatment of black displacement caused by racism and an acquisitive Cajun presence or through his treatment of the individual displacement of characters who leave the world of their birth and become drifters with no communal ties.

In California Gaines took refuge in literature, and through reading hoped to re-create the feeling of belonging he enjoyed in his native region. The Vallejo library was of little assistance, however, for he found no writing that directly addressed his experience or the experience of rural black Louisiana. Accustomed from an early age to hearing the exploits of the people in his parish rendered in oral tales, Gaines keenly felt the want of these stories. In the books available to him the voices he knew so intimately were silent, and the stories they told absent. In the following passage he recalls his forays into the library's holdings and indicates the invisibility of his culture in what might be termed an alien literature:

I read many novels, many short stories, plays—all written by white writers—because there was such a limited number of works at the time by black writers in a place like Vallejo. I found most of the work that I read untrue and unreal to my own experience; . . . I did not care for the language of this writing—I found it too oratorical, and the dialects, especially that of blacks, quite untrue. . . . I did not care for the way black characters were drawn. . . . Whenever a black person was mentioned in these novels, either she was a mammy, or he was a Tom; and if he was young, he was a potential Tom, a good nigger; or . . . a bad nigger. When a black woman character was young, she was either a potential mammy or a nigger wench. For most of these writers, choosing something between was unheard of. ("MJ and I," 26)

The dearth of believable portraits of black Americans and the desire to rediscover the lost voices and tales left in Louisiana became vital shaping influences on the form and subject matter of Gaines's fiction.

Louisiana as a landscape, as a locale nurturing particular ideas and traditions, is ever present in Gaines's writing. In a talk delivered at Southern University in Baton Rouge, Gaines elaborates on his desire to depict vividly, realistically, and sensually the world of his youth:

I wanted to smell that Louisiana earth, feel that Louisiana sun, sit under the shade of one of those Louisiana oaks, search for pecans in that Louisiana grass in one of those Louisiana yards next to one of those Louisiana bayous, not far from a Louisiana river. I wanted to see on paper those Louisiana black children walking to school on cold days while yellow Louisiana busses passed them by. I wanted to see on paper those black parents going to work before the sun came up and coming back home to look after their children after the sun went down. I wanted to see on paper the true reason why those black fathers left home. . . . I wanted to see on paper the small country churches (schools during the week), and I wanted to hear those simple religious songs, those simple prayers—that true devotion. . . . And I wanted to hear that Louisiana dialect—that combination of English, Creole, Cajun, Black. For me there's no more beautiful sound anywhere. ("MJ and I," 28)

All these elements re-create Louisiana in Gaines's literature and emerge in absorbing portraits of human endurance.

Gaines's first effort at writing about his people took the form of an un-published novel, "A Little Stream," penned in a few weeks at age 16. Its plot centered on two black families, one fair and one dark, separated by a stream. With the innocence of a first-time writer, Gaines sent the poorly presented manuscript he had spent all summer typing on a rented type-writer to a publisher who returned it in its original package. Though sad-dened that his dreams for wealth through writing were put on hold, Gaines became determined to write. He wrote and rewrote the work, titled and re-titled it, and eventually, many years later, it evolved into his first novel, *Catherine Carmier.* The enthusiasm that inspired a 16-year-old with no knowledge of the writer's craft to create a novel about his people would de-velop into a talent for reproducing the feel and sound of his community in literature. With subsequent schooling, guidance, and practice, Gaines would masterfully engage his memories of sharecroppers, plantation own-ers, hoodoo women, preachers, and communal traditions to form the sub-stance of his fiction. Drawing so closely upon his remembered past, he would re-create people and a place so familiar to him that both would feel equally familiar to readers.

Gaines remained in Vallejo, where he completed high school, and then attended junior college before being conscripted into the army. The years 1953–55 were spent in military service, and even while performing the du-ties of a private on tours of the South Seas, Gaines wrote during his off-duty hours. After his discharge from the service he enrolled in San Francisco State College, then took odd jobs at the post office and at a printer's office setting type. At San Francisco State Gaines majored in English and continued to write fiction, mostly short stories, his first, "The Turtles," appearing in 1956 in a little magazine entitled *Transfer.* Another short story, "Comeback," earned Gaines the Joseph Henry Jackson Award. Subsequent short pieces appeared in *Southern Writing of the Sixties, Negro Digest,* and *Dark Sym-phony,* to name a few publications. After graduating in 1957 with his B.A., Gaines received the Wallace Stegner Creative Writing Fellowship and began formal study of creative writing at Stanford University.

Study at San Francisco State and Stanford exposed Gaines to the diver-sity of literature and to the possibility of adapting the techniques of literary greats to his own purposes. He saw the equivalency between Turgenev's Bazarov in *Fathers and Sons* and the alienated outsiders he would later cre-ate; in Joyce's Stephen Dedalus he found parallels that would influence his shaping of conflict between secular reason and religious authority; and in Faulkner's Yoknapatawpha he discovered a model for the fictional city, Bayonne, that would provide the setting for all his works.[4]

Gaines balanced his university schooling with his fiction writing and began shaping the ideas present in "A Little Stream," the book he penned at 16, into a novel. He found it difficult to write in San Francisco, however, and hoping a change in locale would stimulate the progress of his work he considered joining friends in Mexico during the summer of 1962. The barring of James Meredith from the University of Mississippi in 1962 unexpectedly changed his plans and instead precipitated his return to Baton Rouge. While recalling the impact this event had upon him, Gaines also describes the influence returning home had upon his writing:

I kept thinking and thinking about this brave, very brave man—and told myself that if James Meredith can go through all this—not only for himself, but for his race (and that included me as well)—then I, too, should go back to the source that I was trying to write about. It was then that I decided to come to Baton Rouge to stay a while and to work. I stayed six months, beginning in January, 1963. . . . I talked to many people, but most of the time I tried listening—not only to what they had to say, but to the way they said it. I visited the plantation that I had tried to write about, while I was in San Francisco. Many of the people whom I had left nearly fifteen years before were still on the plantation. Some were dead, but the ones living could talk about them and did talk about them as though they had simply walked into another room only a few minutes before. ("MJ and I," 31–32)

Going home provided the creative impetus Gaines needed. The experiences he rediscovered upon returning to the Louisiana plantation of his youth gave final shape to his work in progress, and the result when he returned to San Francisco in 1963 was his first published novel, *Catherine Carmier.* The book was originally titled *Catherine,* after a woman he once loved and after Hemingway's heroine in *A Farewell to Arms.* It was renamed upon its publication in 1964. In 1977 *Catherine Carmier* was reissued in Germany as *It Was the Nightingale.*

Reviews and reaction to the novel were rare and often unenthusiastic. It did not receive the critical attention that Gaines's subsequent works would, even though his reputation as a writer was growing. Some reviewers noted the tangential presence of whites within the novel and faulted it for not enmeshing itself in racial politics. What these critics sought was a continuance of the protest tradition adopted by or imposed on many young black writers, and many ignored the very real racial issues Gaines did raise in the context of individual rather than group experience. Others considered *Catherine Carmier* the most pessimistic of Gaines's fictions, and perhaps for this reason it remains largely neglected. The pessimistic tone of the novel,

however, is in keeping with the social determinism that governs the lives of
the characters. Critical reaction might have been more positive were the
book's thematic structure more unified. Often *Catherine Carmier* reads as
two distinct novels, one a love story and the other a story of community traditions and the land. Gaines himself speaks of the duality of content when
he recalls,

In the beginning the novel was twice as long. . . . I had put everything into those
seven hundred pages that I could think of. I wanted everything that I had experienced, that I knew or had heard of about Louisiana . . . house fairs, with gumbos
and fried fish . . . lovemaking, and, of course, there had to be illegitimate children;
there were deaths, wakes, funerals, baptisms, even threats of race violence. . . . But
my editor thought I had a little too much; . . . Stick to the simple love story between the boy from the North and the girl in the South—and leave everything else
out. ("MJ and I," 32)

A Gaines more in control of the written medium would later be able to balance such universal themes as love and individual struggle with the more
particular themes of his Louisiana setting, but this balance was not fully realized in *Catherine Carmier*. The result is a novel that is somewhat uneven
but noteworthy for the masterful rendering of both the physical beauty and
the oral traditions of rural Louisiana.

The two years of Gaines's life following publication of *Catherine Carmier*
were spent in an effort to write a novel about the bohemian life of San Francisco. Perhaps he saw the possibilities of the city and its current atmosphere,
with writers such as Allen Ginsberg and Jack Kerouac creating a literary
renaissance, but he had no feel for the locale, and San Francisco provided no
inspiration for his literature. That the four novels produced from these efforts still remain unpublished attests to the fact that Gaines's real desire was
to write about his native Louisiana.

In 1966 Gaines received a grant from the National Endowment for the
Arts, and in the following year his second novel, *Of Love and Dust*, was
published. An avid record collector, with more than 500 records in areas as
diverse as the European classics, native American music, and jazz, Gaines
was listening to the blues when the theme for *Of Love and Dust* crystallized.
The genesis of this novel demonstrates another strong influence on his writing, and Gaines cites the blues tradition as being as instructive to his work as
any literary example: "I think I have learned as much about writing about
my people by listening to blues and jazz and spirituals as I have learned by
reading novels. The understatements in the tenor saxophone of Lester

Young, the crying, haunting, forever searching sounds of John Coltrane, and the softness and violence of Count Basie's big band—all have fired my imagination as much as anything in literature. But the rural blues . . . is my choice in music." ("MJ and I," 33). The Lightnin' Hopkins blues song "Mr. Tim Moore's Farm" served to inspire two Gaines works, *Of Love and Dust* and the short story "Three Men," in the *Bloodline* collection.

With *Of Love and Dust* Gaines's success as a writer was securely established. Though in some ways this work resembles *Catherine Carmier*—the time of the action is the summer of 1948, and again a novel is set on a plantation along the False River—*Of Love and Dust* received more favorable attention than *Catherine Carmier*, largely because it spoke to the spirit of the times. While *Catherine Carmier* was a very insular novel, exploring the various relationships that existed within a plantation in rural Louisiana, *Of Love and Dust* more directly addressed matters of human rights and racial equality. Though Gaines does distance himself from the protest tradition of the African-American novel, *Of Love and Dust* articulated many of the explosive political issues being vented in the 1960s, particularly the implications of interracial relationships. Reviews of *Of Love and Dust* were largely positive. One reviewer hailed it as "a rare bird, . . . a serious, powerful novel by a talented writer that is accessible to a very wide audience."[5] The enthusiasm of this critic was shared by many, and was indicative of Gaines's ability to appeal to a large audience, one not predominantly black. At the other end of the critical spectrum, many reviewers felt that this novel lacked the maturity and skill of a seasoned writer, that Gaines was still too much in awe of the written medium to control it.

In 1968 Gaines's collection of short stories, *Bloodline*, was released. Many of the pieces were written earlier; three, "A Long Day in November" (1958), "Just Like a Tree" (1962), and "The Sky Is Gray" (1963), predated *Catherine Carmier.* Subsequently, the initial story, "A Long Day in November," was published separately as a children's book, in 1971. *Bloodline* can be viewed as a repository of many of the recurring themes Gaines employs in his full-length fiction, for in all, the quest for black manhood, the reverence of the past, and the value of black life emerge as central concerns. The collection also foreshadows the narrative technique Gaines would rely on in later fiction, the use of many voices to reveal experience, first employed in "Just Like a Tree" and repeated in his last novel, *A Gathering of Old Men.* Using many narrators enables Gaines to depict many actualities, and through these narrators' articulations of experience Gaines experiments with differing perceptions of reality, particularly the reality of black experience in rural Louisiana. He says of this technique so essential to the construction of his fiction,

> I begin with an idea, this point, this fact: some time in the past we were brought from Africa in chains, put in Louisiana to work the rice, cane, and cotton fields. Some kind of way we survived. God? Luck? Soul Food? Threats of Death? Superstition? I suppose all of these have played their part. If I asked a white historian what happened, he would not tell it the same way a black historian would. If I asked a black historian, he would not tell it the same way a black field worker would. So I ask them all. And I try in some way to get the answer. ("MJ and I," 38)

Diverse voices enrich *Bloodline* with a communal narrative that vivifies the nature of rural Louisiana's oral tradition.

Many critics viewed *Bloodline* as confirmation that Gaines had mastered the art of short fiction, and his genuine depiction of everyday struggles to maintain dignity impressed most as being original. Though many reviews addressed the quest for manhood present in most of the stories, Gaines's use of African-American cultural forms remained largely unacknowledged. It was not until later works were published that preserving the oral tradition and other African-American cultural constructs would be noted as a profound motivation for Gaines's works and as an influence on his style.

In 1971, after the appearance of *Bloodline*, Gaines was writer-in-residence at Denison University in Granville, Ohio. During this period he devoted most of his time to forming what would be his most critically acclaimed work, *The Autobiography of Miss Jane Pittman*. Elaborating on Aunt Fe, the central character in "Just like a Tree," Gaines crafts a fictitious autobiography that actually serves as a cultural biography. The accessibility of Jane's character, as well as the breadth and verisimilitude of her experience, secured his reputation as a significant African-American author.

Gaines has said that he began composing *The Autobiography of Miss Jane Pittman* as early as the days spent on the porch of his Louisiana home listening to, talking to, or writing letters for the older people of his parish (an action he would later replicate in the novel through the character of Jimmy Aaron). *Miss Jane* continues his chronicling the temperament of his quarters and casts communal history as a microcosm of larger American experience. In recalling how he gave form to the novel, Gaines indicates his desire to incorporate an inclusive vision of American history in the story of one woman's life:

Alvin Aubert, who used to teach at Southern University—Al and I were talking one day, and I asked him to name ten or twelve very significant things to have happened in Louisiana since the middle of the nineteenth century. Al began with the Civil War. . . . Then he went to the Reconstruction Period. He also said he thought the floods of 1912 and 1927 were very significant. He mentioned the construction of the spillways to control floods, he mentioned Huey Long, he talked about the Civil Rights Movement, and he also mentioned athletes like Jack Johnson, Joe Louis, and Jackie Robinson.

Al Aubert was not the only person of whom I asked these questions. I went to several other people, older than Al, and uneducated, and asked them the same thing. ("MJ and I," 35)

The experiences Gaines received in this manner, coupled with information garnered through extensive research, were shaped into the core incidents of Jane's life. In structuring *Miss Jane* he gave thought to using the multiple narrative he employed in "Just like a Tree," having the novel begin on Jane's burial day with people gathered to recall their memories of her, and through personal recollections unfold a history of the South. He changed his approach, however, when he became so fond of the central character that he wanted no other voice but hers to reveal her life and its events.[6]

Reviewers were quick to praise *Miss Jane* for wedding "social protest" to "human interest" without sacrificing the art of writing. The balance Gaines was able to strike between art and polemic fostered a universal appeal most evident in his no longer being referred to as a fine black writer, but as a fine southern writer. The widespread popularity of *Miss Jane* was such that CBS aired it as a movie in January and November of 1974, but its production fueled great debate about the capability of a white-controlled medium to treat black life and history appropriately. Though Ernest Gaines was a key consultant during the production's making, the fact that a white writer, Tracy Keenan Wynn, created the screenplay, replaced Gaines's black history teacher with a white feature reporter, and changed the presentation of some significant events raised questions about the preservation of the work's authenticity. Gaines, however, while admitting that the necessity of wedging a book into a two-hour format dictates editing out some of the work's nuances, was satisfied with the effort. Later the novel was translated into Japanese and Russian.

After *Miss Jane* Gaines received a Guggenheim Fellowship for 1973–74. He began an as-yet-unpublished work, "The House and the Field," but turned instead to write *In My Father's House*, which was published in 1978. The theme of this work, the gap between fathers and sons, is one Gaines had wanted to explore even before the writing of *Miss Jane*. He describes this motif as a "pet theme," for which he gives the following background: "We know that on the slave block in New Orleans, or Washington, D. C., or Baltimore, or wherever the slave ships docked, families were separated. Mothers were separated from their children, . . . fathers from their sons. . . . I feel that because of that separation they still have not, philosophically speaking, reached each other again. I don't know what it will take to bring them together again. . . . I don't know that the father . . . can reach out and bring his son back to him again. . . . Anyway, that is the main theme that is running through the new novel—*In My Father's House*."[7]

Though *In My Father's House* is Gaines's shortest book, it was the longest in the making, and his greatest difficulty—crafting an authentic voice while employing the omniscient point of view—caused the flaws some critics cited within the book. Gaines himself said of the book while it was in progress, "From the omniscient point of view, it is harder for me (for the characters to take over), because it seems that I'm always interrupting them. . . . It slows the novel down too much; it impedes the progress, the movement. Quite often it throws things out of the line in which it travels; form gets in the way of development." (Rowell, 41). Some critics agreed with Gaines and felt this novel lacked the direction and voice present in his earlier works, citing the jolting shift in narrative tone between the objective observations of the novel's first half and the more introspective descriptions of its second half. On the whole, however, critical review was favorable. Though Gaines's departure from his traditional rural setting and his use of the omniscient narrator cause some unevenness within the novel, *In My Father's House* is a moving psychological study.

With *A Gathering of Old Men* Gaines restores rural Louisiana as a setting, but the action unfolds in the 1970s. The contemporaneity of the novel is barely noticeable, however, because social change comes slowly in this parish. *A Gathering of Old Men* also restores Gaines's use of many narrators telling a story, and with this thematic and stylistic "coming home" Gaines returns to his strengths as a writer. As with *Miss Jane*, Gaines saw a second novel made into a highly praised television movie, airing in May 1987. The controversy over authenticity that plagued *Miss Jane* was not repeated, perhaps because rendering the memories of many aged black males necessitated a vision more in keeping with Gaines's original, or perhaps because Charles Fuller, the black playwright who created both *A Soldier's Play* and the screenplay for the movie version, *A Soldier's Story*, wrote the television screenplay in close keeping with the original novel.

Reaction to this novel was almost as uniformly enthusiastic as that to

Miss Jane. Some reviewers found the novel's lack of conscious "art" a flaw. Many felt that Gaines's reproduction of the spareness inherent in oral narrative left too much for the reader to visualize. Such comments, however, ignored the tradition that primarily propels Gaines. The leanness of his narrators' accounts descends from his recollection of storytellers who needed to provide little elaboration because they shared a community of meaning with their listeners. In his world and the world of his novel, histories are told and retold from person to person, from generation to generation. Within this oral continuum a silent second text gives unspoken meaning to stated meaning.

Critical acclaim for Gaines's writing culminated in 1987, when the American Academy and Institute of Arts and Letters presented him with one of its annual literary awards. The academy's recognition indicated a growing public awareness of the importance of Gaines's writing not only to black American readers but to any reader interested in the southern mind. Even though Gaines has spent most of his adult life in northern California, where he currently lives in the predominantly black Fillmore section of San Francisco, it is rural Louisiana that impresses his literary imagination, and he makes yearly sojourns there to maintain the cultural ties that bind him. His experience chopping cane for 50¢ a day on the plantation; the complex relationships that exist among the black, white, Cajun, and Creole communities; and the life of Baton Rouge, the larger city close to his parish, constitute his literary world along the St. Charles River. That Gaines can reproduce his world so clearly in his writing can be credited not only to his own vivid recollection but also to the stories of others who lived in the locale for many years before him. Their graphic chronicles become his as he molds their oral tales into literature.

Gaines's most direct conduit to the world that would later form the quintessence of his work is the aunt who reared him while he was still in Louisiana, Miss Augusteen Jefferson. Gaines recalls his aunt and her world this way: "She was a cripple and could not go visiting, so people came to visit her. I'd be there to serve them ice water, or coffee. There was no radio, no television, so people *talked* about everything, even things that had happened 70 years earlier. I learned about storytelling by listening to these people talk."[8] Gaines would use the stories he heard on his aunt's porch to construct the major characters and themes of his fiction. His aunt, who died in 1952, was not only a viaduct to a cultural reservoir but also the model for later characters whose moral strength compensated for physical handicaps and allowed them to achieve whatever goals they set.

Gaines listened carefully as his elders told stories of black displacement by the Cajuns who settled rural Louisiana shortly after slavery. Under share-cropping, many blacks were dislodged from the land they had worked for generations when the former plantations were inequitably redistributed. Cajun farmers, because they were white, received the plots that would yield a better harvest, while black farmers were left the lesser bottomland.[9] The casting of the Cajuns as both an element of negative change and the repre-sentatives of a new southern order replacing the old reflects the influence of an author whose style Gaines greatly admires, William Faulkner. The un-stoppable Cajuns bear a strong resemblance to Faulkner's Snopes clan, and present in almost all Gaines's works, they are a breed apart, looked upon by blacks as usurpers and by the decaying southern gentility as rapacious arrivistes.

Gaines also credits Faulkner with influencing the structure of his lan-guage and dialogue. In an interview he states, "I have learned as much from Faulkner's language—handling of the language of both Blacks and the Southern whites—as from anyone else. . . . I have no interest in Faulkner's philosophy. I could no more agree with his philosophy no more than I could agree with [former Alabama governor] Wallace's. But this man taught me how to listen to dialogue; he taught me how to leave it out. You can say one word and if you say it right and build up to it and follow through, it can carry as much meaning as if you had used an entire sentence."[10] Like Faulkner, Gaines weaves the complex psychological relationships left by slavery into a dominant motif. His fiction explores many considerations, among them the devaluation of black life (often illustrated through black men who must seek their manhood, or black women who have been victi-mized by whites), the peculiar race and caste systems of Louisiana, and the ambivalence of slaveholders' descendants who are now burdened by their legacy.

A second major literary influence on Gaines has been the Russian writers of the nineteenth century. Seeing a parallel between Russian peasantry and black Americans, Gaines has stated, "If the Black man is not the peasantry of this country, then there is no peasantry. And no matter what you do and no matter who the writer is, sooner or later he deals with the peasantry of a country. The greatest writers of every country have dealt with the peasantry of that country" (Beauford, 16). Gaines admired the sympathetic realism and believability with which writers such as Turgenev and Tolstoy painted their peasant world, and found these to be in sharp contrast to the mostly shallow depictions of the African-American "peasantry" by white southern writers: "Their peasants were not caricatures or clowns. . . . They were peo-ple. . . . They could be as brutal as any man, they could be as kind. The

American writers in general, the Southern writer in particular, never saw peasantry, especially black peasantry, in this way; blacks were either caricatures of human beings or they were problems. . . . [T]hey were very seldom what the average being was. There were exceptions, of course, but I'm talking about a total body of writers, the conscience of a people" ("MJ and I," 27). Gaines wants his "peasants," like those of Turgenev's *Sportsman's Sketches*, to be realistic representations, rather than two-dimensional caricatures. Like Turgenev, he does not idealize his rural characters, and they encompass the range of human heroism and frailty. In the same way Turgenev uses the experience of Russian peasants to argue the injustices of the feudal system, so does Gaines use the dignity of his characters to expose the unfairness of his plantation world.

Though Gaines admits to a variety of literary influences, his main influence has been his native community. He uses his elders and their stories to ground himself securely in a particular folk past, and the presence of this past is felt no matter what subject or period he addresses. His belief that to deal with the future, one must be aware of the past is evident in a series of photographs that form his photo essay "Home," among them the quarters of River Lake Plantation; the house where he was born; Miss Jane's tree in Lakeland, Pointe Coupée; his church that also served as a school; the cane field; and the road Baton Rouge.[11] Even though he emerged as a writer during the turbulence of the civil rights and black nationalist movements, Gaines's ties to his past are the strongest influence on his fiction. What is important for him are his cultural roots and the oral stories that perpetuate them. He chronicles a transitional Louisiana moving from the decay of slavery to the uncertain future portended by the civil rights movement, and even contemporary material is sifted through the sieve of the past.

Some have criticized Gaines for not addressing the pressing changes of this period, but his distance from social upheaval imbues his work with a timeless appeal. He has never been considered a "protest writer," for he is less concerned with explaining the adversity of the black experience to an outside audience than with showing how individual characters find the courage to surmount personal adversity. As he told an interviewer, "Too many blacks have been writing to tell whites all about 'the problems,' instead of writing something that all people, including their own, could find interesting, could enjoy. And in so many cases they leave out the humanity of their characters" (Desruisseaux, 44). It is precisely this essential humanity that Gaines seeks to portray in each of his works.

Gaines's solution to the tension of art versus protest in literature is the creation of quiet heroes and heroines modeled on the people of his parish.

The mettle of his Aunt Augusteen, a woman who refused to feel sorry for her condition, helped to frame the rectitude of the strong but not necessarily vocal leaders who appear in his work. Like Augusteen, these characters did effect change, not through rhetoric but rather through hard work, ensuring the next generation's access to greater advantages. Gaines's emphasis on individual strength is similar to Ernest Hemingway's, and in an interview he speaks of his admiration for Hemingway in the following manner: "I've always liked the way he understated things, and I admire his writing style, which told me I did not have to use adjectives and adverbs, and that's the damn truth. Also, he wrote about people who always came through gracefully under pressure. Now *nobody* has experienced as much pressure as the black in this country, and nobody has come through more gracefully" (Desruisseaux, 44). Maintaining dignity and self-esteem under negative circumstances is a constant theme in Gaines's fiction, and any consideration of race and history will be evoked through the motives and experiences of individual men and women.

The importance of intimate human stories to Gaines is evident in every aspect of his writing, from theme to narrative technique. He so fully envisions a character that he feels them, hears them, and absents himself as omniscient narrator: "Once I develop a character and 'hear' his voice, I can let him tell the story. My writing is strongest when I do that. In most cases when my books are giving me a hard time I am not using *that* voice but my own, the omniscient narrator, the voice of God looking down on things" (Desruisseaux, 13). When we read both Gaines's fiction and his comments on his art, it becomes evident that the voices he "hears" as he writes are the voices found in his native Louisiana. His characters adopt the cadences, dialect, and expressions of this rural region as they spin yarns of human affliction and triumph. They voice the sentiments of their music: the resignation of the blues, the determination of the spirituals, the ambiguity of jazz. They retell the black folk legends of John Henry and Singalee Black Harriet.[12] They respond to the call of the preacher's sermon, while sprinkling the root powder of the hoodoo woman. Their voices reverberate through his canon as their life experiences become the music of his text. Gathering their voices, Gaines acts as an African-American *griot*, singing their praises and preserving their moments in his literature.

Chapter Two
The Odyssey to Self in *Bloodline*

My men are always standing like they're waiting to go through a door.
— Ernest Gaines

Of the Louisiana memories that inform Gaines's fiction, one, the denial of manhood, shapes everything he writes. Often in his world, black men were not allowed to be men, and he offers this theory as to why: "[T]he blacks who were brought here as slaves were prevented from becoming the men that they could be. They were to be servants of the whites, nothing more. A *man* can speak up, he can do things to protect himself, his home and his family, but the slaves could never do that. . . . These things happened even after slavery" (Desruisseaux, 44). In Gaines's world being a black man meant constant struggle, whether to gain basic subsistence or to maintain positive self-worth. Gaines transforms the daily quests for manhood he witnessed in Pointe Coupée into literary quests, and nowhere is such transformation more evident than in *Bloodline*.

The short stories collected in *Bloodline* can be viewed as a series of doors, each opening onto a greater awareness of the meaning of manhood. In all but the last story, boys and men pass through portals of evolution in search of self-realization. Whether young or old, each of the central characters undergoes metamorphosis: from innocence to awareness, from victim to actor, from rootlessness to rootedness, from life to death. Though written at different points during his career, the stories can be more deeply understood when viewed as a connected whole, a bildungsroman depicting a quest toward manhood and stressing the importance of family and community in the making of dignity.

In *Bloodline* Gaines takes the universal theme of the quest found in literature as diverse as myths, folktales, and epic poetry and particularizes it to the experience of men in his Louisiana world. The characters on his odyssey surmount the challenges of family dissolution, segregation, and dehumanization, and their gateways to manhood are knowledge of community and culture. Each story of the quest is given to a particular narrator, and for each Gaines carefully creates vision, perspective, voice, and language appropriate to the storyteller's age. The collection begins with stories told by boys—the first by a six-year-old struggling to understand the relationships among personal, familial, and communal identities; the second by an eight-year-old who must learn to maintain his self-worth as he leaves the safety of his quarters for the unknown peril of a segregated city. The next two stories depict more mature men on the verge of manhood, one attempting to create a positive identity and one seeking acceptance for his identity in an inhospitable society. The final story, a communal narrative, departs from the theme of seeking manhood and celebrates the importance of traditions in the maintenance of a community's identity. The tales encompass experience from childhood to old age, and recurring motifs transform separate stories into a larger odyssey toward human dignity.

Of Fathers and Sons

In the opening story of *Bloodline*, "A Long Day in November," the young narrator, Sonny, chronicles a day with his father. The apparent simplicity of subject matter is misleading, for the story details the coming-of-age of both father and son. In crafting the story, Gaines admits to the influence of both James Joyce and William Faulkner. Of having the story's events take place in one day, Gaines says, "I got Joyce's . . . *Ulysses*, the 'Let's do it all in one day,'"[1] and in the course of a day, Sonny watches his father make order out of disorder, transform despair into hope, and ultimately realize what it means to be a father and a man. The language of Sonny's first-person narrative resonates with the rhythms of a child's speech, and Gaines credits *The Sound and the Fury* with suggesting the tone of the story: "In the first part of Faulkner's *Sound and Fury*, the Benjy part, Benjy uses the simplest terms to express his feelings: 'the gate is cold,' 'the fire is good,' 'I stamped my shoes on,' all this sort of thing. This childlike section is so convincing that I really fell in love with it" (Gemmett and Gerber, 334). The innocence of Sonny's language highlights his vulnerability and accentuates the isolation and searching for place that characterize the short story. He is a lone persona, very aware of himself and his personal sensations, attempting to find security in a tenuous and sometimes threatening environment. His description of awakening reveals the removal he feels from the world, his desire to shut his eyes to it, and his sense of foreboding as he realizes he must become part of it: "Somebody is shaking me but I don't want to get up now. . . . It's warm under the cover here, but it's cold up there. . . . It's warm under here, and it's dark, because my eyes's shut."[2] When his mother shakes him to remind him to go to the outhouse, Sonny's long day in November, his journey to find identity and place, begins. As he accompanies his father through the day, he moves from introspection to external observation and learns how to value self, family, community, and culture.

Sonny's early observations are given from the insular safety of his warm bed. The security of the womb is evoked as his thoughts focus first on those things most immediate to his own personal sensations of coldness, warmth, and waking: "I don't want to get up, because it's cold up there. The cover is over my head and I'm under the sheet and the blanket and the quilt. It's warm under here" (*BL*, 3). His observations continue, gradually expanding outward with the realization of being "home," along with the acknowledgment of his mother's presence. At this point the element of familial identification creeps into his awakening thoughts: "I don't know who's calling me, but it must be Mama because I'm home" (*BL*, 3). Finally Sonny's observations incorporate his external surroundings: "I can see the big pecan tree over by the other fence by Miss Viola Brown's house" (*BL*, 5). His description, moving from the inspection of inner sensation to the acknowledgment of outer environment, signals the start of outward quest for identity and family unity.

The story's plot centers on the marital problems of Sonny's mother, Amy, and his father, Eddie. Amy resents the growing attention Eddie pays to his automobile. While for Eddie his car is a symbol of masculinity and freedom within a society that traditionally has denied both to black men, Amy views it as an intruder usurping the attention Eddie should give to his family. In a larger sense the car becomes a symbol of those aspects of a technological culture which further draw society away from more humanistic values.[3] Because of Eddie's neglect Amy leaves him, takes Sonny, and returns to her mother. The body of the story details Eddie's attempts to reunite his family. As Sonny's parents separate and his father makes him part of his quest to regain his wife's affection, Sonny watches Eddie reconstruct paternal identity through an awareness of self, family, and the true meaning of being a man.

An integral part of being a man, the story argues, is being a father. At the beginning of Sonny and Eddie's odyssey, neither father nor son has a clear conception of the patriarchal role. When his father asks Sonny to reveal how much love he has for each parent, Eddie is essentially asking Sonny to bolster a fragile paternal self-esteem:

> "You love your daddy?" he says.
> "Uh-huh," I say.
> "That's a good boy," he says. "Always love your daddy."
> "I love Mama, too. I love her more than I love you." (*BL*, 15)

Central to Sonny's conception of himself is the relationship he shares with his parents, but as the story develops it becomes evident that he particularly needs a secure relationship with his father to develop a healthy manhood. A recurring theme in Gaines's canon is injected at this point, the importance of father-son lineage in the formation of male identity. In an interview Gaines has addressed the need for paternal presence and familial unity by stating,

"I was raised by a stepfather. My mother and father split up very early—and it is a theme that enters everything. . . . I don't know where the fathers are. . . . The son was separated from the father on the auction block and they have been looking for each other since. . . .

Son and mother have always sort of been there. Because let us take for example the white father who rapes the Black woman. No matter what happens, the child was the product of the mother. The father never had to look after the child. The mother had to look after that child. So that the child would always be with the mother. That is why the boy and the mother are always together in my books." (Beauford, 18)

The historical antecedents of the black father-son relationship influence all Gaines's father-son pairs. The severing of paternal lineage during bondage manifests itself in the gap he sees between fathers and sons in the present. Affiliation with either an actual father or the concept of the father motivates many of his male characters as they seek to define themselves as men within a patriarchy, and Sonny is no exception. Though he knows his mother well enough to believe he loves her more than he does his father, to make his self-definition whole Sonny needs to come to terms with his father and understand the implications of what is essentially Eddie's quest for manhood. In Gaines's vision "the son becomes the father" (Beauford, 18), and Sonny's self-definition and entry into manhood will depend upon an intimate knowledge and understanding of Eddie.

While being party to his father's attempts to cement the family, Sonny also learns the importance of community in the formation of male identity. The teacher and older students who provide encouragement when he, from anxiety, wets himself; Freddy Jackson, who attempts to replace Eddie in Amy's affection; Johnny Green, who tells Eddie where to go for counsel in his attempts to win Amy back—all contribute to leading Sonny and Eddie to manhood. The two communal elements most responsible for Eddie's maturation and the subsequent familial reunification it brings about are the local preacher and the hoodoo woman. It is interesting to note that Gaines uses two elements of black religious thought as key representations of the larger community. Often in conflict, these distinct religious figures have persisted side by side as integral parts of black spiritual philosophy, and each has become a charged symbol.

Most churches, even from the time of slavery, provided more than religious sustenance to black Americans: they provided an outlet to political and social power. In some, slaves secretly learned the fundamentals both of Christianity and of reading and writing. Later many became axes for civil rights activities. In his history of black religious activity during slavery, Albert J. Raboteau gives insight into the breadth of the church's function in black culture: "An agency of social control, a source of economic cooperation, an arena for political activity, a sponsor of education, and a refuge in a hostile white world, the black Church has been historically the social center of Afro-American life."[4] While the church was the social center of African-American life, the preacher was the center of the church's existence. Both religious leader and cultural institution, the preacher articulated and chronicled a people's aspirations and despair. The role of this remarkable religious icon is well documented, but nowhere more eloquently stated than in W. E. B. Du Bois's *The Souls of Black Folk*: "The preacher is the most unique personality developed by the Negro on American soil. A leader, a politician, an orator, a 'boss,' an intriguer, an idealist,—all these, he is, and ever, too, the centre of a group of men, now twenty now a thousand in number. The combination of a certain adroitness with deep-seated earnestness, of tact with consummate ability, gave him his preeminence, and helps him maintain it."[5]

Complementing the preacher as spiritual leader is the hoodoo or conjure practitioner.[6] He or she has held an equal, if not as overtly recognized, place of power within black culture. Deeply rooted in African religious traditions, hoodoo and conjure practitioners have been the connective between the black New World and the Old.[7] Acting as interceders among human beings, a pantheon of deities, and unknown spiritual powers, they influence the destinies of their petitioners through the use of roots, powders, potions, and divining. Raboteau is again helpful in understanding the role of these spiritualists: "Like Christianity, conjure was a system of belief, a way of perceiving the world which placed people in the context of another world no less 'real' than the ordinary one. . . . [T]he conjure doctor had the power to 'fix' [induce calamity] and to remove 'fixes,' to harm and to cure. . . . Variously known as root doctor, hoodoo doctor, two-facer, and wangateur (from *ooanga*-charm), he was respected and feared by those blacks and whites who had implicit faith in his power" (Raboteau, 275–76). Such systems of belief as hoodoo provided viable alternatives to the Christianity of the slave master, giving slaves the power to create a world order distinct from the servitude inherent in the religion of slavery. Gaines's juxtapositioning of the minister and hoodoo practitioner as Eddie encounters each foreshadows a recurring theme in his fiction, the impotency of orthodox religion.

Looking at Gaines's treatment of traditional religious leaders, we recognize his shaky faith in organized religion. He has said in an interview, "I don't think religions solve anything. It's good to believe. . . . For you to survive you must have something greater than what you are, whether it's religion or communism, or capitalism. . . . But as of right now, I don't think orthodox religion has solved anybody's problems" (Ingram and Steinberg, 343). Gaines's sympathies seem to lie with figures and practices rooted in the folk culture of his native Louisiana. In "A Long Day in November" and in subsequent works, he neutralizes the potent icon of traditional Christian faith, the minister, and juxtaposes him to a powerfully rendered symbol of non-Christian belief, the hoodoo woman. Through this symbolic relationship orthodox religion often emerges as an opiate useful in bemoaning woe and placating anger but subordinate to a nonorthodox belief steeped in a more individual spiritual ethic.

Gaines further contrasts spiritual traditions by juxtaposing a male character and a female character. That the figure of authority and action in this episode is a woman, and that she is set in opposition to a man whose complacency restrains his capacity to act, is part of a larger pattern that establishes itself in Gaines's work. Consistently in his canon, men seek while women do. His women provide the steadying influence that balances the restlessness, rebelliousness, or resignation of the men in his fiction, and it is they who are the catalysts for subtle but certain change. It is not surprising, then, that when Eddie desires aid in resolving his problems with Amy, he must ultimately go to the hoodoo woman for concrete assistance.

Believing in traditional Christian doctrine, Eddie is initially inclined to turn to the preacher of the quarters for aid. Sonny describes the preacher, and we soon learn that his help will be ineffectual: "Me and Daddy go inside and I see Reverend Simmons sitting at the fireplace. Reverend Simmons got on his eyeglasses and he's reading the Bible. He turns and looks at us when we come in. He takes off his glasses like he can't see us too good with them on, and he looks at us again" (*BL*, 40). The preacher's gesture of removing his eyeglasses and looking again is an example of Gaines's subtle characterization. Through a simple action he evokes the preacher's inability to "see" Eddie's problem clearly enough to offer assistance.

Eddie's minister proffers complacency rather than providing counsel. When petitioned to plead Eddie's cause before Amy and her willful, outspoken mother, the reverend exhibits what Gaines portrays as the passivity of orthodox religion—ineffectual placation and compliant resignation. After a minimal effort he insists that Eddie leave his life in God's hands, saying, "I got to get on back up the quarter. Got to get my wood for tonight. I'll see you people later. And I hope everything comes out all right. . . . I tried, son. . . . Now we'll leave it in God's hands" (*BL*, 44). The hands in which Eddie's fate is actually left are the more capable hands of the hoodoo woman, Madame Toussaint. The following passage articulates his disillusionment with orthodox religion and reveals a dejected Eddie, reluctant to turn to non-Christian beliefs but aware of where true assistance will be found: "When you want one of them preachers to do something for you, they can't do a doggone thing. . . . Nothing but stand in that churchhouse and preach 'bout Heaven. I hate to go to that old hoo-doo woman, but I reckon there ain't nothing else I can do" (*BL*, 44). In addition to assisting Eddie's attempt at reconciliation, Madame Toussaint adds the dimension of the ancestral folk past to his quest for manhood. She personifies history, as represented through her bearing the name of the black freedom fighter Toussaint-Louverture. Through a spiritual tradition brought from Africa and transformed in the New World she provides cultural continuity, and in reunifying Eddie's family she provides a familial continuity that symbolically reverses the historic rending of black families Gaines cites as an influence in his treatment of fatherhood and manhood.

For a fee, Madame Toussaint consults her spirits and advises Eddie on how to proceed to cement his family. After succinctly defining his problem, that he is neglecting his wife and son for a car, and tersely providing a solution, "You want your wife back?. . . Then go set fire to your car. . . . You can't have both" (60), she brings about the reunion of Eddie and Amy, and their family remains sound. She teaches Eddie that an automobile does not make a man; maintaining familial stability does. Sonny learns, also, by watching Madame Toussaint, and though she is at first a frightening figure he subsequently comes to view her as a natural part of communal identity.

As the episodes of Sonny's day continue to unfold, they are linked by descriptions of the natural surroundings. Using images of the landscape to connect the various phases of a character's development is a technique Gaines will employ repeatedly, most evidently in his first novel, *Catherine Carmier*. The uncertainty of Sonny's day-long quest is counteracted by the stability of nature. The sky, trees, and cane field anchor him as he drifts along on his father's odyssey. To mark his awareness of place in the world he focuses on those familiar elements of his natural surroundings which provide a feeling of security: "I can see the fence back of the house and I can see the little pecan tree over by the toilet. I can see the big pecan tree over by the other fence by Miss Viola Brown's house. . . . They got plenty of stars in the air, but I can't see the moon. There must be ain't no moon tonight. The grass is shining—and it must be done rained" (*BL*, 5). Emerging as a silent presence, nature provides Sonny and other characters with cover and protection, placement and reference.

With the natural world marking the various stages of his self-knowledge, Sonny's day eventually comes to a close. Witnessing the steps Eddie has taken to maintain his identity as a father and as a man gives him a vocabulary of impressions with which to articulate his own nascent identity. The result is a Sonny more sure of himself and his place in the world. The isolated and uncertain "I" that began the story is bolstered by story's end with a "we" that joins Sonny to his family and community as all gather to watch Eddie set fire to his car and assume the role of patriarch: "I look down the headland and I see Uncle Al and Gran'mon, and all the other people coming. . . . They come where me and Mama's standing. . . . We stay there a long time and look at the fire" (*BL*, 71–72). The community's positive response to Eddie's act shows that he has indeed become a man:

> "Never thought that was in Eddie," somebody says real low.
> "You not the only one," somebody else says.
> "He loved that car more than he loved anything."
> "No, he must love her more," another person says. (*BL*, 72)

Because Eddie's quest is complete, so is Sonny's. Both have endured isolation, weathered painful experiences of fragmentation and alienation, and arrived at an appreciation of the security true manhood provides: for Eddie it is the security that stems from the new regard with which his wife, mother-in-law, and community view him; for Sonny it is the security of knowing his family will remain intact.

Eddie's self-realization gives Sonny new confidence, and Sonny's self-assurance is evident in his thoughts as he drifts off to sleep: "I go to sleep some, but I open my eyes again. . . . I hear Mama and Daddy talking low. I like Mama and Daddy. . . . Daddy ain't got no more car now. . . . I know my lesson. I ain't go'n wee-wee on myself no more. Daddy's going to school with me tomorrow. I'm go'n show him I can beat Billy Joe Martin shooting marbles. . . . Us house smell good. I hear the spring on Mama and Daddy's bed" (*BL*, 78–79). Sonny's review of the day's events displays his heightened esteem for his father, an esteem he may intuit from his family and community now seeing Eddie as a stronger man and father.

Rather than loving his mother more than his father, he now loves "Mama and Daddy" equally. It can also be noted that in going to Sonny's school Eddie no longer forsakes his son's education for an immature infatuation with a car. Sonny's final comments contrast sharply to those beginning the story, and the anxiety in his opening description gives way to serenity when he notes, "It's some dark under here. It's warm. I feel good 'way under here" (*BL*, 79). Though he expresses sensations identical to those which start the story, watching his father's development allows Sonny to feel part of a protective rather than threatening environment. Instead of closing his eyes to a cold daylight, he opens them to the warmth of his dark, familiar surroundings.

"A Long Day in November" is characteristic of Gaines's ability to take the simplest elements of human experience, a day in the life of father and son, and transform them into a moving fiction. The accounts of Sonny's interactions with his parents, the meals he eats, the abc's he learns—these evolve into a larger tale of the quest for a dignified identity. Eddie's emergence into manhood foreshadows Sonny's ultimate course and suggests an endless succession of complicated journeys to pride and self.

Survival with Dignity

"The Sky Is Gray," the second story in *Bloodline*, resembles "A Long Day in November" in its theme of quest for identity, manhood, and place. The narrator is again a boy, James, who undertakes a journey to self-realization. Like its predecessor, the story moves from the smaller environment of family to the larger environment of community, and the narrator again travels with a family member. Here the similarities end, for the stories do represent not a parallel but a progression: from innocence to awareness.

In "The Sky Is Gray" James is accompanied on his odyssey by his mother. The absence of a paternal figure can be seen as a manifestation of the absence of father threatened in "A Long Day in November." With no father present, James must more quickly learn how to become a man and, in a sense, assume the roles of both son and father, caring for himself, his siblings, and his mother. His circumstances place him at a point further along the path to manhood than is the case with Sonny, and his journey develops a theme explored in the two upcoming stories, societal devaluation of the black male identity.

"The Sky Is Gray" unfolds primarily in the town of Bayonne, a more ominous environment notably different from the safe, rural quarters of "A Long Day." The movement of the innocent from rural simplicity to urban complexity roots the story in the bildungsroman tradition, and James's entry into awareness is marked by an increasing intricacy in narrative tone. The childlike expression that characterized Sonny's story is gone, and a more mature narrative voice takes over. Though the language of "The Sky Is Gray" consists of the simple sentences and repetition characteristic of a child's speech, more complex sentences are used to construct James's narrative, and his observations reveal a growing cognizance of life's nuances and an understanding of his mother's teachings.

James's quest begins with a trip to the only dentist in his area who will treat blacks. Gaines has stated that Eudora Welty's "A Worn Path" influenced the writing of this work, and the stories are similar in several ways. The determination of Welty's narrator, Phoenix, who overcomes hardship and monthly walks miles along a well-trodden path to Natchez seeking medicine for her grandson, is shared by James and his mother as they encounter difficulties in their determined resolve to make a better life. The sureness with which Phoenix navigates the country roads disappears once she enters the overwhelming city, and there is a similar overpowering in "The Sky Is Gray" as James leaves the security of his quarters and enters the more threatening locale of Bayonne. Finally, Phoenix's refusal to relinquish dignity despite the social conditions that label her a "charity" medical case is paralleled by Octavia's desire to teach James that being a man means maintaining dignity at all costs.

Where six-year-old Sonny had only to venture out into his own quarters and watch his father's quest for self, eight-year-old James must traverse a more complex urban landscape if he is to reach the freedom of manhood. A ride on the bus where he passes "the little sign that say 'white' and 'colored'" and a walk past a café where he sees whites eating while he must stand outside, hungry, are the malevolent signposts that replace Sonny's naturalistic markers of trees and cane fields.[8] James leaves a black world whose rules he understands; moves through a transitory world where "the river is gray" and "the sky is gray"; and enters a white world whose antagonism is indicated by many images, one of which is the Confederate flag replacing the American flag in front of the courthouse, an institution assumed to symbolize "justice for all." The self-knowledge James acquires is thus deeper than Sonny's, producing an understanding of both manhood and blackness. As a young black man negotiating a menacing environment, James must develop those skills which will ensure the survival of his dignity and self-worth, for only these will guarantee him control over his emotional life. His trip to the dentist becomes an odyssey on which he learns the cunning necessary to eke out self-respect within his society. He must be prepared for his voyage at an early age, and his preparation begins with the stern schooling of his mother.

A woman whose husband has been taken away by the army, Octavia is rearing a family on her own and is concerned that James learn the most important lesson of his environment, that one does what one must to survive. In one instance she punishes him when he is unable to kill two pet redbirds for the family's supper. Concerned that James be able to take care of himself and his family should the need arise, she knows she must teach him that subsistence is more important than the sentiment he holds for the birds. Octavia's attempts to edify him are successful, and he becomes keenly aware that suffering seems a constant element of his existence. His understanding of this principle is indicated in his stoic refusal to acknowledge fear or pain, even when faced with the excruciating pain of a toothache. To admit to either is to acknowledge weakness, and a young black man, fatherless in an unsympathetic society, "can't ever be scared and . . . can't ever cry" (*BL*, 84). As James proceeds to the dentist he is tested on how much of his mother's schooling he has digested. Three incidents serve as landmarks along James's road to self-mastery: his overhearing of a conversation between a college student and a minister, his watching his mother maneuver their separatist social system for his benefit, and his viewing an interchange with an old couple who own a small grocery store.

Waiting in the dentist's office, James overhears a conversation between a young man attending college and a now-familiar character in Gaines's work, a preacher content to abide by the status quo. The young man trusts neither the symbols nor the rhetoric of American democracy and "questions every stripe, every star, every word spoken" (*BL*, 95). His polished appearance in suit and tie, his educated manner, and his ability to use language to confound his verbal opponent instill awe in James and cause him to affirm, "When I grow up I want be just like him. I want clothes like that and I want keep a book with me, too" (*BL*, 100). As he did in "A Long Day in November," Gaines juxtaposes the force for change this young man represents with a resistant force, an ineffectual preacher who is the tool of a manipulative religion. When the young man eloquently attacks the preacher's antiquated philosophy by saying, "A white man told you to believe in God . . . to keep you ignorant so he can keep his feet on your neck" (*BL*, 97), James hears passive religious acceptance indicted as an opiate numbing black sensibility to the necessity for change. When he witnesses that the preacher, unable to respond verbally to the young man's criticism, discards his professed pacifism and strikes his adversary (who ironically is the one to "turn the other cheek"), James's admiration for the young man is reinforced as he sees nonviolence practiced rather than merely preached.[9] His bearing teaches James that a man can quietly assert his point and maintain his dignity, and James now considers education as a viable means of escaping the demeaning confines of his environment.

The knowledge that he need not succumb to negative social definitions is only part of the information James will need to survive in the segregated environment of Bayonne while maintaining self-respect. When the dentist adjourns for lunch without seeing him, he and his mother are left to wander the streets in the bitter cold. Unable to buy food because of their poverty, and forbidden to enter the warm shelters in the area of the dentist's office because of their color, they become rambling outcasts in a society in which the whim of any white is empowered to affect their destiny. While they wait for the dentist to reopen his office, Octavia must devise ways in which she can keep James from the cold and at the same time carefully adhere to strict rules of racial separation. Observing his mother manipulate their environment moves James closer to what will be his particular entry into manhood, the psychic freedom that comes from emotional self-mastery. In one instance Octavia enters a white-owned hardware store and pretends to inspect ax handles for purchase while James heats himself at the wood stove. Her dissembling enables her to warm him without compromising her dignity by begging the proprietor to allow her son use of the stove. Here, hiding her true feelings and motives, she makes use of the technique of "masking" and teaches her son a valuable lesson in pride and survival.[10]

James's odyssey in Bayonne culminates in an episode that amplifies his appreciation of the importance of maintaining dignity. When an elderly white couple attempt to help him and his mother by feeding them and giving them temporary shelter, he witnesses his mother and the woman perform an intricate dance as each discreetly circles the other in their offering and acceptance of help. The women respect each other's situation, and each is cognizant of the importance of pride to the other. Together they design a strategy in which the woman feeds Octavia and James and, in return, James is made to take out garbage cans that he suspects are empty. In partaking in this complex masquerade and in witnessing his mother's subsequent refusal to take no greater an amount of salt pork from the woman than she is able to purchase, he again sees that a large part of achieving manhood is maintaining the pride that sustains it. James learns another lesson, however, one revealing the universality of Gaines's themes: that artificial polarities that divide the world along lines of black and white are often complicated by compassion and shared human experience.

The journey to Bayonne has a marked impact on James, and his growth is evident in the manner in which he perceives his mother and her motives. Whereas in the beginning of the story he saw only her severity and fear-inducing authority, by the story's end, after watching her stymied by segregated circumstances, he sees her vulnerability. The severe limitations placed upon her actions by her environment take form in the image of her walking through the city not knowing which way to go, and this image is rendered through James's eyes: "We go on up the street. Walking real slow. I can tell Mama don't know where she's going" (*BL*, 103). His comprehension of her financial constraints is visible in his reluctance to have her spend money to feed him even though he is hungry: "I hope she don't spend the money . . . on me. I'm hungry, I'm almost starving I'm so hungry, but I don't want her spending the money on me" (*BL*, 109–10). Finally, in his regarding his mother while he eats, James's maturation becomes evident in his transition from a boy cared for by his mother to a young man who will some day care for her: "I look at her. . . . She's looking real sad. I say to myself, I'm go'n make all this up one day" (*BL*, 110).

James's avowal to "make all this up one day" comes from an internalization of his mother's teachings and from his memory of the young man whose poise offered another alternative to survival in a world that emasculates him. His odyssey through Bayonne has been a crucial element in his development and growth, teaching him to discern the threats his segregated society poses for him and offering remedies to cope with and diminish its menace. By the end of the story, when his mother simultaneously admonishes and observes, "You not a bum . . . you a man" (*BL*, 117), he knows his journey to manhood and self-worth has culminated.

Both "A Long Day in November" and "The Sky Is Gray" are universal stories of quest for identity and manhood. In the second story, however, the quest is complicated by considerations of race. The events of James's odyssey unfold because he cannot immediately see the only dentist in Bayonne who will serve blacks. Many of the difficult choices he and his mother must make are complicated by color barriers. His space is clearly demarcated by narrow separatist practices, and his journey gives him the experience to form knowledge that will insure his psyche against devaluing confinement. These considerations particularize the universal story of the quest, and the placement of this story signals the increasing presence of racial themes within the collection. The individual transcending a hostile environment and ultimately asserting a manhood independent of societal devaluation emerges as a key theme in the next two stories of the collection and in later Gaines works.

Liberation through Incarceration

The seeds of subtle humiliation Gaines sows in James's story mature into
a systematic degradation in the two that follow. Moving from the experiences of young boys to those of young men, the successive pieces explore the
quest for black manhood and identity at later stages, and as they do so focus
on two major motifs in African-American expression, the expendability of
black life and the complexities of miscegenation. From the slave narrative to
recent fiction, the worth of black life and the social implications of biracial
interaction are steady currents in African-American writings, and Gaines
treats each in "Three Men" and "Bloodline."

In "Three Men" the central character and narrator, Proctor Lewis, volun-
tarily confesses to killing a man in self-defense. What makes his gesture so
unusual is that no one expects him to turn himself over to the authorities or
pay for his crime, because the life he has taken is that of another black and
thus, in his society, worth very little. Indeed Proctor admits his guilt only
because he is certain he will be released to the custody of the white owner of
a local plantation and allowed to substitute fieldwork for a prison sentence.
Through Proctor's eventual transformation as he realizes that his attitude
and plan of action reinforce a system that devalues black life, Gaines explores the issue of black expendability.[11]

In Proctor's society black life is an inconsequential entity. Early in the
story, as he stands in the sheriff's office waiting for attention, he describes
the law enforcers' reaction to his presence in a way that indicates his negligi-
bility: "They looked at me, but when they saw I was just a nigger they went
back to talking like I wasn't even there" (BL, 121). The sentiments behind
the phrase "just a nigger" are those Proctor must fight if he is to attain dignity and self-esteem, and they have their origins in the institution of slavery
whereby blacks were perceived as merely chattel. In a stroke that recalls the
slave origins of black devaluation, Gaines consistently employs metaphors
and similes that liken human beings to animals or objects while constructing
the revelations that transform Proctor.

When Proctor's cell mate—the sage, cynical, and aged Munford
Bazille—describes the value of black life in their society, he figuratively
equates blacks with brutes and thereby accentuates the tragedy of
dehumanization: "[A] nigger ain't worth a good gray mule. Don't mention
a white mule: fifty niggers ain't worth a good white mule" (BL, 141). The
analogy is reminiscent of Frederick Douglass's account of the dividing of his
master's estate: "I was immediately sent for, to be valued with the other
property. . . . We were all ranked together at the valuation. Men and

women, old and young, married and single, were ranked with horses, sheep, and swine. There were horses and men, cattle and women, pigs and children, all holding the same rank in the scale of being."[12] The reminder of the slave experience adds timelessness to Gaines's story by underscoring the manner in which black humanity has traditionally been denied. The use of animal metaphors further underscores Proctor's transformation from what is essentially an unthinking brute with no concern for the value of human life to a rational man who deems human life as worthy.

Tragically, Proctor has accepted black degradation as a given. The man he has killed is "nobody," merely someone he shot in a fight over a woman who means nothing to him. Accepting society's deprecation of his blackness, he feels no remorse, and all his actions are governed by this acceptance. In a telling example, when he turns himself in and is asked for identification, he checks his instinct to retrieve the necessary papers from his wallet. A racist decorum forbids him to obtain forthrightly even those personal articles which document who he is; instead, he must defer to the whites who essentially still have mastery over his being: "I got my wallet out my pocket. I could feel T.J. and the other policeman looking at me all the time. I wasn't supposed to get any papers out, myself, I was supposed to give him the wallet and let him take what he wanted" (*BL*, 122). Proctor's credentials, like his person, are the property of whites, and his survival depends upon his knowing the rigid rules of race and caste. Though he is well schooled in yielding to whites, Proctor must learn the lessons of self-respect that Gaines's other male characters have learned. Like Eddie, who has Madam Toussaint, and like James, who has his mother, Proctor also has a mentor—in the form of Munford—to guide him to a positive manhood. Munford becomes his surrogate father, and through articulation of his own experience teaches Proctor that to be a man he must value his own life and, by extension, black life in general.

Munford's first step in educating Proctor is to explain to him that the diminishing of black manhood they now confront is part of a complex process beginning at birth: "It start in the cradle when they send that preacher there to christen you. At the same time he's doing that mumbo-jumbo stuff, he's low'ing his mouth to your little nipper to suck out your manhood. . . . But they don't stop there, they stay after you. If they miss you in the cradle, they catch you some other time. And when they catch you, they draw it out of you or they make you a beast" (*BL*, 140). The beast allusion accentuates the essential dehumanization at the core of black devaluation, and Munford complements his insightful analogies with autobiographical details describing the manner in which white humanity is maintained at the expense of black: "Been going in and out of these jails here, I don't know how long. . . . Forty, fifty years. Started out just like you—kilt a boy just like you did last night. Kilt him and . . . got off scot-free. My pappy worked for a white man who got me off. At first I didn't know why he had done it. . . . Didn't wake up till I got to be nearly old as I'm is now. Then I realized they kept getting me off because they needed a Munford Bazille. They need me to prove they human—just like they need that [toilet] over there" (*BL*, 137).

In Proctor, Munford sees himself—the same history, the same circumstances. In Proctor he also sees one last chance to break the cycle of devaluation, if not for himself then for a younger generation of black men. Munford knows what Proctor must learn; that the most lamentable aspect of black disparagement is the internalization of this depreciation by blacks themselves. Proctor and a younger Munford are convinced of their lack of worth and thereby fulfill the prophecy of black worthlessness. By continually being bailed out of jail and permitted to kill again, their belief in their own importance and the importance of others is eroded. Only an acknowledgment of black worth, manifested through the desire to pay for the taking of a black life, can break this cycle. To free himself from the routine of release and return to prison, Proctor must reevaluate the significance of his life and larger black life.

Proctor fears incarceration because it symbolizes an end to his conception of freedom—the freedom to drink, fight, and enjoy women. As he regards the sere Munford and the effeminate Hattie, who shares their cell, Proctor envisions confinement as leading to the deterioration and emasculation he perceives in them. With Munford's help, however, he realizes that freedom has a variety of interpretations, and as his conception of its symbolic meaning changes, so too does his conception of prison. When he discerns Munford's import, Proctor comprehends that the debt he would owe the plantation owner, Medlow, should he secure his release, is a far more consequential shackle. To sycophantishly "bow and say, 'Yes, sir,' and scratch my head," Proctor observes, would mean "[H]e'd have me by the nuts . . . and I'd have to kiss his ass if he told me to" (*BL*, 145). Only going to prison will free him from Medlow's control. Proctor remembers Munford's admonition, "[Y]ou don't go to the pen for killing the nigger, you go for yourself. . . . You go, saying 'Go fuck yourself, Roger Medlow, I want to be a man. . . . For once in my life I will be a man'" (*BL*, 141). Ironically, incarceration becomes the liberation leading to Proctor's manhood.

Munford's teachings begin a process of introspection alien to Proctor, and his reflections reveal both his fear that the process of devaluation is too advanced to be checked and his determination to halt it: "Maybe I'm a' animal already. . . . Hell, let me stop whining; I ain't no goddamn animal. I'm a man, and I got to act and think like a man" (*BL*, 144). What crystallizes Munford's counsel, and what actually inspires Proctor truly to "act like a man," is a 14-year-old cell mate who forces him to reevaluate his own life and finally to accept the knowledge Munford gives him.

Just as Munford sees himself in Proctor, Proctor sees himself in the adolescent and ultimately develops a feeling of fatherliness toward him. At this point the significance of the title "Three Men" is expanded. Through most of the story the title refers to the three men occupying a cell, Hattie, Munford, and Proctor, and foreshadows Proctor's adopting qualities of both Munford and Hattie—Munford's acumen and Hattie's warmth—to create a new definition of what it means to be a man. Though Munford is the character who most extensively counsels Proctor, Hattie's influence is essential to Proctor's revising his notion of manhood. Initially Proctor finds Hattie's homosexuality repulsive. Watching the kindness Hattie administers to the youth, however, changes Proctor's assessment, and the traits he once equated with effeminacy he now sees as indicative of compassion. Hattie teaches him how to respond to others in a humane manner. Coupling the knowledge of Munford and the compassion of Hattie in his dealings with the youth, a new Proctor emerges, and the title of his story comes to signify the passage of wisdom from the generation of Munford and Hattie, parental symbols effecting Proctor's renaissance, to a second generation, which Proctor represents, and finally to a third, in the figure of the young cell mate. Thus the element of family so crucial in the Gainesian quest for self manifests itself as three men share the lessons of three generations on becoming a man and maintaining self-respect in a society that encourages neither for a black man.

As he attempts to protect the youth and guide him away from making the same mistakes he has made, Proctor by his caring engenders a new understanding of self and black worth while strengthening his resolve to insist on punishment for his crime. Toward the story's end he vows, "I knowed I was going to the pen now. . . . Even if Medlow came to get me, I wasn't leaving with him. I was go'n do like Munford said. I was going there and I was go'n sweat it and I was go'n take it. . . . I wanted to stand. Because they never let you stand if they got you out" (*BL*, 152). Proctor's new consciousness renders the closing scene of the story particularly touching. After his cell mate has been beaten by the authorities and returned to his cell, Proctor cleans his bruises and gives him comfort. As he describes his actions, saying, "I wet my handkerchief and dabbed at the bruises" and "I washed his back good and clean" (*BL*, 154–55), he is indeed a man. He has learned the value of his own life and come full circle from being a young man who kills indiscriminately to being a young man who now attempts to nurture.

Like Sonny, Eddie, and James, Proctor learns what constitutes true manhood. He makes a choice, at great personal cost, not to continue a pattern of debasement, and his stance is no less than a liberating redefinition of black worth as precious and inestimable. An acknowledgment of his own and others' valuable humanity becomes central in his quest for self and the emergence of his manhood.

The Prodigal Son

As the theme of odyssey to manhood is developed throughout *Bloodline*, each quest becomes increasingly more impeded, each route a little less direct. In James's and Proctor's cases, being a member of a marginalized race complicates the search, yet each has discovered or created a network of mentor and family to assist in the quest. Copper Laurent, the main character in the collection's title story, "Bloodline," cannot readily find such a network, because he is the son of a white landowner and a black sharecropper. While the title "Bloodline" may imply flow and connection, its implications become ironic in Copper's case, wherein familial continuity is checked by values of race and Copper is left a solitary character groping for self-definition.

Copper has returned to the plantation on which he was born to claim his birthright as his father's only direct surviving heir. As much as a birthright, he seeks validation of his identity. Neither claim is recognized as legitimate, however, because of his biracial parentage. His bloodline is in effect severed. He cannot regain a family, as can Eddie; he has no mother to guide him, as does James; and he does not create a surrogate family, as does Proctor. Copper's familial heritage is one of dissolution in which his mother is exploited by his father and his stepfather is rendered impotent. His description of his family history shows Copper to be a victim of racial conventions that fragment families: "I always knew who my father was. . . . But I knew I couldn't say a thing about it. It would have gotten me in trouble, and probably gotten my mother in more trouble. . . . Two years after we left here, my mother died. . . . My suppose-to-be father, who had been too nutless to say I wasn't his while we lived in the South, kicked me out of the house before my mother was cold in her grave. He was not going to support any white man's child" (*BL*, 212). Copper is the innocent victim of a triangle that encourages the exploitation of black women and the downgrading of black men. His splintered family provides no sanctuary along a quest for self complicated by being neither black nor white.

Often when handled in literature, the experience of miscegenation that forms Copper's background has symbolized the psychological fragmentation that derives when one's identity must be aligned between two races.[13] In African-American literary works, such miscegenation has also taken on the added significance of representing the hypocrisy of a racist society that on the one hand condemns interracial relationships, while on the other condones the sexual exploitation of black women by white men. In both treatments, the product of biracial unions was most likely drawn as a tragic mulatto, and at first glance Copper's characterization seems descended from this legacy. Gaines reimagines this figure, however. Though he incorporates aspects of traditional uses of miscegenation in Copper's quest for self-affirmation, his characterization negates Copper's likeness to the tragic mulatto so frequently found in such works as Harriet Beecher Stowe's *Uncle Tom's Cabin* or William Wells Brown's *Clotel; or, The President's Daughter,*[14] and described by Alvin Aubert in the following terms: "The mulatto's anguish, his 'tragedy' according to the literary stereotype, derives from his being neither white nor black, neither 'eagle' nor 'crow' in a society in which the difference is crucial, particularly for the isolated individual."[15] Although he hovers precariously on the edge of insanity, at times rendered delusional by straddling two racial allegiances, Gaines's Copper bears only a surface resemblance to this literary figure. He does not evoke pathos but rather stands as a symbol of change. Though the story of Copper's quest borrows sentiments from literature about the tragic mulatto, ironies of racial lines so blurred they are no longer distinct are treated with touches of humor. Readers do not perceive Copper as a wretched victim who elicits their sympathy for his lack of racial identification; instead, his comments prompt them to observe the senselessness governing the rules of black and white interaction. He signals the advent of a theme that will be dominant in Gaines's later work, the effect of change on a static social order. A Faulknerian influence is again evident here as the Laurent family joins the Sartorises, Sutpens, and Compsons in watching a New South replace the Old.

In the southern setting of "Bloodline," the absence of the slave order renders racial conventions meaningless and forces characters to create new self-definitions based not solely on race. Copper and his paternal uncle, Frank, who now owns the land Copper claims, share an antagonism because the rules of their society say they must, but as "Bloodline" progresses, their similarities begin to upstage their differences and force the reevaluation of the

labels that define them. In his article "Hearing Is Believing: The Landscape
of Voice in Ernest Gaines's *Bloodline*," John F. Callahan sums up the irony
that governs Frank and Copper's relationships: "[W]hatever the horrors and
injustices of Southern history, the essential connections between people of
both races have been maintained through kinships of blood and experience."[16] The unique interaction between southern blacks and whites established a racial bond, and often a familial bond, in which two polarized
groups had to use each other to construct definitions of themselves, yet had
to simultaneously acquiesce to social convention by denying the existence of
such a bond. Though both Copper and Frank tacitly acknowledge the truth
of Copper's assertion "[L]ike it or not, I'm a Laurent" (*BL*, 215), their rigid
society continues to reinforce the black narrator Felix's observation that
Copper is "the wrong color to go round claiming plantations" (*BL*, 160).
Since their blood transcends racial lines, Frank and Copper share a history
more important than race, and their fight is one not only of black against
white but of blood against blood.

While Copper's society defines him as a black man, he clearly thinks of
himself as a Laurent, and therefore if not white, then certainly not black.
Throughout, the story suggests that he is more Laurent and more imperious
than even his uncle Frank. Felix, the caretaker of the plantation, character-
izes Copper's bearing as more akin to the descendant of slaveholders than to
the descendant of slaves: "He didn't talk to me like he was talking to a' old
man, he spoke to me like he was speaking to a slave" (*BL*, 204). It is interesting to speculate on the subtle switch of the verb in Felix's statement as
talk is substituted for *speak*. Perhaps we can read the change as indicative of
two possible modes of communication that might exist between Felix and
Copper: one in which Copper talks with Felix, giving him the respect due
an elder in a shared culture, and the other in which Copper speaks to him as
a slave, denying respect and accentuating the cultural rift Copper's white
ancestry fosters. That Copper chooses the latter accentuates the wide gulf
that separates him from his black kinship, while insinuating the unacknowledged likeness he seeks to share with his white relatives.

In striking contrast to Copper is his uncle. Frank Laurent's demeanor is
that expected of a landowner and southern gentleman but is far more relaxed and informal than his nephew's and indicative of his deteriorating belief in his social authority. Though Frank is left the family plantation, he
finds the inheritance of land and family name burdensome. Fatigued by
maintaining the legacy of racial inequity, Frank nonetheless feels bound by
his larger identity to defend the status quo and gives the following rationale:
"I didn't write the rules. I came and found them, and I shall die and leave

them. They will be changed, . . . and soon, I hope. But I will not be the one to change them" (199). In spite of Frank's feeble defense, the existing social order is eroding. Copper's presence presages a new one, and within it new identities will have to be defined. While this is a story of Copper's quest for identity, it is vital to remember that his identity must be defined in relation to Frank's, and Frank's, in turn, must be redefined in relation to Copper's. Their interdependency symbolizes the futility of blacks and whites who have lived in such close contact for so long attempting to define themselves independently of each other.

As "Bloodline" develops, a deterioration of meaningful racial demarcation unfolds through a variety of means, the most marked of which is the juxtaposing of Frank and Copper and the shifting societal forces each represents. Copper's vitality is in sharp relief to Frank's ill health, and like Frank, everything associated with the Laurent plantation is in a state of decline: the niece who will inherit the estate once Frank dies and who is expected to see to the maintenance of class conventions will defy family tradition and parcel out the land to eager Cajuns for sharecropping, thus beginning an irreversible dilution of Laurent money and power; the blacks on the plantation, who have fundamentally supervised its operation, have now "overstepped" the boundaries of traditional racial mandates, making decisions on the plantation without consulting Frank; and finally, the weary Frank must attend to the appearance of a nephew of biracial heritage demanding the plantation as his right. His summoning of Copper in an effort to discharge him from the plantation actually constitutes Frank's last endeavor to maintain the class and racial supremacy ingrained in his social conceptions.

With each successive attempt to evict Copper comes an undermining of Frank's authority, the values he represents, and ultimately his identity. When he assigns a black worker the task of bringing Copper to him, the deference the worker shows to Copper's black aunt, Amalia, in the following interchange exemplifies Frank's eroding power:

"Go down there and bring him back up here," Frank said. "I don't want any scars on him, . . . but I want him up here."

"Yes Sir," Little Boy said. Then he turned to 'Malia. "Hope that's all right with you, Miss Amalia?" . . .

"You're asking *her* if it's all right when *I* told you to do something?" Frank asked him. . . .

"Do like Mr. Frank say," 'Malia said, with her head down.

"Just a minute," Frank said. "Who the hell's running this place, me or Amalia?"
(*BL*, 173)

Gaines's subtle humor magnifies the inappropriateness of archaic racial
rules in an order that can no longer sustain them. Just as it is unclear who
now runs the plantation, it is also unclear why Copper cannot be a legitimate heir to it.

No matter how Frank attempts to remove Copper, and the metamorphosis he portends, he will not be moved or denied. When Frank sends another set of men to secure him, Copper sends them back to Frank tied in a
chain. Frank's reaction is riddled with disbelief, prompting Felix to observe,
"I'm sure he thought we was doing all this to either run him crazy or kill
him" (179). When yet another man sent to apprehend him returns bloodied and pities Amalia "for having a crazy nephew on her hands" (197), the
pointlessness of Frank's attempt to "break" his own kin and tenaciously
hold on to a decaying system is again humorously underscored. Although
"Bloodline" recalls earlier literary models that stressed the tensions between
racial identification and familial kinship, Gaines's comic touches transform
the tragedy of miscegenation into a farce of racial prejudice.

Ultimately Frank must acknowledge that the past is dying and that
Copper's appearance signals the start of a new era. Eventually, though
Copper does not succeed in attaining the inheritance he has come for,
he does compel Frank grudgingly to call him "nephew" and admit the
injustice done to him. Toward the end of the story, he prophesies the
future in his statement "Your days are over, Uncle. . . . It's my time
now" (*BL*, 217).

In Copper's time family lineage will supersede considerations of race. In
attempting to secure his legacy, he does so not only for himself but for
"millions . . . without homes, without birthrights" (*BL*, 213). His quest is
to reconstruct the bloodlines that racism severs, and as such, his odyssey
differs from the more personal quests undertaken by the protagonists in
the first three stories. His manhood will be realized through the creation
of not only identity but also social acceptance for the disenfranchised. Perhaps because his vision is so grand, the degree of his success remains uncertain at story's end. His closing remark to his uncle—"Tell my aunt I've
gone. But tell her I'll come back. And . . . when I do, she'll never have to
go through your back door ever again" (*BL*, 217)—raises the question,
Did Copper achieve the goal of his quest? The ambiguity of the ending
casts "Bloodline" as the most pessimistic story in the collection. Unlike the
previous protagonists who arrived at their goals of self and manhood,
Copper seems unfulfilled in his quest and remains a character still waiting
to "go through a door."

The Future in the Past

"Just Like a Tree" is both finale and prelude. It resonates the motifs of the stories before it and sounds the upcoming strains of later works. It enlarges upon the theme of quest for manhood and personal identity by expanding the import of these terms, making them applicable to the existence of a larger community. If in earlier stories manhood meant an assertion of personal dignity despite all obstacles, in this culminating story manhood now connotes an assertion of cultural dignity and a demand for equality. If previously personal identity meant a character's realization of the nature and worth of the self, in this story identity comes to mean those elements which join many and create a community. By reflecting on the central character, Aunt Fe, many characters are able to define what makes communal dignity and what connects it to cultural pride.

"Just Like a Tree" tells the story of Aunt Fe's uprooting from the quarters she has been a part of all her life. She seldom speaks in the story, but her presence is undeniable, as it motivates characters and generates the story. Her example and teachings have inspired some younger members of the community to partake in the civil rights movement and demand equal treatment. The result of their demands is a retaliatory bombing, killing a woman and her two children. Fe's family now fear for her security and have decided upon measures to move her to the North, where they believe she will be safer. On the eve of her departure, the community comes to pay tribute to her.

The story's structural conception is informed by Faulkner's *As I Lay Dying*.[17] In that book Faulkner creates a pastiche narrative focused on a loss, the death of a mother, and moves the story forward in chronological time by dividing it into sections of monologue given by 15 characters, each having a different perspective on the action and reality presented in the novel. Gaines uses multiple narrators in a similar vein to recall the life of Aunt Fe and memorialize her. It is a technique he will rely on in subsequent works, particularly *A Gathering of Old Men*. Perhaps *As I Lay Dying* inspired Gaines not only because of its structure but also because it is essentially a folktale circulated among a community of characters and recalling a delayed burial. In this sense its conception is very much in keeping with Gaines's desire to craft a story inspired by the rich oral tales of his native Louisiana.

As Gaines's 10 narrators speak out one by one, the piece becomes a gathering in which experience is both remembered and ongoing. Through talking and telling, "Just Like a Tree" relates one woman's history, a

community's history, and ultimately a culture's history. Each character contributes to the account, moving it forward in time, and each is given a distinct voice and language with which to reveal his or her remembrances.
History is recalled by "talking," but as "talk" is used within this story it signifies more than the act of speaking or telling a story: it encompasses self-
affirmation; it commands respect; and it creates communal identity.

In the "James" narrative section of the story, the speaker makes an observation on the importance of talk in the culture and community of "Just Like
a Tree." When he observes of the people, "All they know is talk, talk, talk"
(BL, 230), he indicates the capacity to talk to bind diverse people in a collective cultural memory. A northerner and a self-styled hipster, James sports
a wig and is removed from the roots of his southern culture. His language is
littered with the slang of the northern metropolis. He views rural southern
blacks as "lame," "primitive," "way-out cats" and cannot understand their
traditions and values, or Fe's significance, referring to her merely as "the old
chic." Perhaps precisely because he is an outsider, James's insensitive objec-
tivity inadvertently gives a lucid portrait of the act of talking and what it
means to this community. His description of the range of people gathered to
pay tribute to Fe indicates the medley of communal vision that will emerge
in "Just Like a Tree": "I look in the front room where they all are. I mean,
there's about ninety-nine of them in there. Old ones, young ones, little ones,
big ones, yellow ones, black ones, brown ones" (BL, 231).

The communal importance of talk and the discrete voice of each character represent the many visions that went into the making of this community's identity: from the innocence of the young boy, Chuckkie, to the jive of
James, to the stoicism of Aunt Fe and Aunt Clo. As each narrator speaks,
his or her remembered moments of Fe's history illuminate larger episodes of
African-American history. Presaging what he will accomplish later in *The
Autobiography of Miss Jane Pittman*, Gaines allows one woman's life to represent the larger epic of African-American folk history. Since Fe's story is actually a concentration of key aspects of black American history, Gaines
appropriately begins "Just Like a Tree" with a passage from the spiritual
that gives the story its name.

Spirituals were the first musical form to weave the cadences of African
musical expression to the language and religious conceptions the slaves were
taught when brought to the United States. They were also among the earliest African-American creations to preserve the links between Africa and
black America while articulating African-American experience. In his history of slave religion, Albert Raboteau notes that slaves, "drawing from the
Bible, Protestant hymns, sermons, and African styles of singing and danc-

ing, . . . fashioned a religious music which expressed their faith in folk songs, . . . hybrids, born of mutual influence and reciprocal borrowing between traditions."[18] Titling this story after a spiritual accentuates its role as symbolic connective and reveals the power of oral traditions to cement the folk history of a people.

Like a spiritual, Fe connects the members of her community to their past, and her presence houses their collective identity. Every narrative voice is related to her in some context, whether as actual kin or as friend. As the narrator Leola's comments make evident, Fe represents the family, the spiritual striving of her people, and the core of the community: "Aunt Fe, Aunt Fe, . . . the name's been 'mongst us just like us own family name. Just like the name o' God. Like the name of the town—the city. . . . Aunt Fe, Aunt Fe" (*BL*, 227). Leola's analysis of Fe's name indicates Fe's symbolic import as the community uses her to construct its definition.

The narrative voice that gives the most insight into how remembrances of Fe act as communal and cultural definition is Aunt Clo's. Her recollections are united by an extended tree metaphor, and she says of the loss of Fe, "You get a big hole in the ground, sir; and you get another big hole in the air where the lovely branches been all these years" (236). The analogy is appropriate, for Fe holds her "folk" together, preventing the erosion of familial and cultural ties.

Clo's tree metaphor further suggests a comparison between Fe's uprooting and the larger historical cleaving of African-American roots. Her vivid personification of a tree as Fe makes the following description a stunning image of the removal of black Americans from their homeland: "Be just like wrapping a chain around a tree and jecking and jecking, and then shifting the chain little bit and jecking . . . some in that direction, . . . and then pulling with all your might. . . . Then you hear the roots crying, . . . and you jeck and jeck on the chain, and soon she start to moving . . . but if you look over yo' shoulder one second you see her leaving a trail" (*BL*, 235–36). As the story develops, it becomes apparent that the trail left by Fe's rending is composed of fond recollections that symbolically allude to larger episodes of African-American history. Imbedded in Clo's description of Fe's upcoming fate, for example, is a reference to the historical episode of black migration.

Clo speaks of the existence awaiting Fe in the North and tangentially addresses the negative impact migration has had upon rural southern blacks who journeyed north in the hopes of discovering greater freedom and opportunity: "The North to me, sir, is like the elements. It mystify me. But never mind, you finally get there, and then you try to find a place to set [Fe]. You look in this corner and you look in that corner, but no corner is good. . . . So finally, sir, you say, . . . 'I guess we'll just have to take her to the dump'" (BL, 237). The tragedy Clo predicts for Fe was a continual tragedy in African-American history, one befalling many slaves seeking freedom in the North only to find it an illusive ideal and one later befalling migrant blacks who transplanted themselves and their families to the North only to find they had traded the poverty of the rural South for the poverty of the northern ghettos. Her characterization of the North's inability to fulfill aspirations additionally implies that black southerners must seek actualization where their roots lie, in the South. Gaines will further develop this emphasis on the importance of native place to identity in *The Autobiography of Miss Jane Pittman*.

While for Aunt Clo Fe's presence provokes reflection on black displacement, for Anne-Marie Duvall, the only white narrator in the story, it generates introspection into the complex interaction of the black and white races. Fe is as much a psychic cornerstone for Anne-Marie as she is for the other black characters. A servant in her household since the time of her grandfather, Fe is "family" to and cultural preserver for Anne-Marie. Because she has been so close to Fe, and because she can make no sense out of the necessity for her leaving, Anne-Marie, through her thoughts, reveals the confusion wrought by the inequality permeating racial interaction. Her narrative adds an integral element to the history of this community and shows that this communal and cultural identity is composed of both black and white.

As she makes her way through a driving rain, attempting to visit Fe for the last time, Anne-Marie must follow roads as treacherous and obscure as the rules she must follow in crossing racial lines. Her trip is taxing and causes her to observe the following:

She lives far back into the fields. Why? God, why does she have to live so far back? . . . But the answer to that is as hard for me as is the answer to everything else. It was ordained before I—before father—was born—that she should live back there. So why should I try to understand it now? . . .
    . . . The lightning flashes just in time to show up a puddle. . . . But there's no light to show up the second puddle, and I fall flat on my face. For a moment I'm completely blind. (BL, 240–42).

Both Anne-Marie's inability to see and her stumbling aptly represent her perplexity as she strives to account for the racial order that forces Fe to live in the hindmost section of the fields, where the worst land had been reserved for blacks to sharecrop. Like Frank Laurent, she finds it easier to uphold conventions "ordained" before her time and discordant to her feelings for Fe than to risk the emotional complexities of change. Her urges to disregard traditions are like flashes of lightning, briefly illuminating a path to racial equity and then disappearing, leaving the darkness of complacency. The rain continues to fall, and Anne-Marie continues vainly to derive sense from the animosity that caused the bombing necessitating Fe's removal: "That was too bad about the bombing—killing that woman and her two children. That poor woman; poor children. What is the answer? What will happen? What do they want?" (*BL*, 241). Her questioning of the immediate violence within the sheltered community gathers momentum and addresses larger issues, "What do they want?" and future questions, "What is the answer?" The answers to these questions are ones Anne-Marie does not necessarily want, however, preferring to remain comfortable in her ignorance.

Not all of Anne-Marie's recollections are tainted with the negative aspects of racial relationships. Her fondness for Fe documents the positive affiliations that often endured despite practices that discouraged them, and her true affection for Fe is evident in her description of the last time she will see Fe's face: "I look into that wrinkled old face again. . . . And I lay my head in that bony old lap, and I cry and I cry" (*BL*, 243). Her dogged determination to see Fe before she is taken away and to give her a remembrance, along with Fe's gentle response to her, exhibits a caring relationship that persists in spite of racial malevolence.

Anne-Marie's narration reveals the difficult relationships caused by institutions of the past and foreshadows the complexity of future relations described in the narrative section "Etienne." The matter-of-fact tone of the narrative voice in "Etienne" is appropriate for the introductory portion of the section, an interpretation of the history of race relations. The vision of this explanation is at once reminiscent of biblical prose, as the genesis of racial hatred is recounted, and Marxist, as the divisive class and economic system that perpetuates it is analyzed:

It started a million years ago. It started when one man envied another man for having a penny mo' 'an he had, and then the man married a woman to help him work the field so he could get much 's the other man, but when the other man saw the man had married a woman to get much 's him, he, himself, he married a woman, too, so he could still have mo'. They start having children—not from love; but so the children could help 'em work so they could have mo'. But even with the children one man still had a penny mo' 'an the other, so the other man went and bought him a ox, and the other man did the same. . . . And soon the other man had bought him a slave to work the ox. . . . But the other man went out and bought him two slaves. . . . And soon they had a thousand slaves apiece, but they still wasn't satisfied. (*BL*, 244)

The philosophy presented in "Etienne" fuses many schools of thought, and the voice of this section is a universal one, neither overtly young nor old, male nor female. It is appropriate that a voice capable of keen analysis and encompassing so many interpretive visions acquaints us with the motives of the character Emmanuel, the activist whose demands for civil rights set in motion the violence that now jeopardizes Fe's safety.

Many in the community blame Emmanuel for Fe's fate, but Etienne's insights into the manipulations that accompany the system of racism clearly show who is at fault. The greatest portion of the section is devoted to an account within an account, as Emmanuel discloses that Fe is the motivation behind his activism. By telling him of his personal family history and, by extension, disclosing a common occurrence in his race's larger history, Fe has made Emmanuel realize that desire for retribution must be transformed into desire for change. He reveals her impact on him when he explains to her the impetus behind his actions: "I love you, Aunt Fe, . . . but I'm not going to stop what I've started. You told me a story once, Aunt Fe, about my great-grandpa. . . . Remember how they lynched him—chopped him into pieces? . . . I was so angry I felt like killing. But it was you who told me to get killing out of my mind. . . . You were right. We cannot raise our arms. Because it would mean death for ourselves. . . . But we will do something else" (*BL*, 246–47). Emmanuel's sentiments show Fe to be more than a repository of the past: she is a vital influence in forming the future. Because she is an immediate representation of communal and cultural history, she becomes a symbol of leadership for Emmanuel. The traditions, principles, and values she represents inspire him to integrate the past as he forges a future for his people.

As all the narrative sections illustrate, Fe is so integral to her community's psychic survival that her moving constitutes a threat to its spiritual continuity. In a story that stresses the connections of the present to the past, however, Fe appropriately does not move, but dies in her community. The final scene of the story occurs between two contemporaries, Aunt Lou and Aunt Fe. Both these women are like the old oak trees of Gaines's Louisiana that have weathered the elements and emerged as symbols of endurance. In a rare instance in the story, we actually hear Fe's voice, and her words are few as she tells her oldest friend, Lou, "I feel like singing my 'termination song'" (*BL*, 249). Rather than be moved from her home, Fe seems to will and welcome death. Her song trails off, as does her life, and Fe dies, "calm, calm,

calm," according to Aunt Lou. "Just like a tree that's planted 'side the water" (*BL*, 221), she will not be moved from the community in which she is so rooted and whose very identity she defines.

Fe unites all the characteristics Gaines sees as necessary to a healthy identity, whether personal or cultural: an unflinching dignity, an appreciation of past and family, and solid placement within the sanctum of community. Though she dies at story's end, her spirit permeates all his canon, felt each time a character makes a heroic stance for self-validation.

The Pilgrim's Progress

All the stories within *Bloodline* are tales of quest, of characters traversing the difficult path to positive identities. Though the stories were written at different points in his career, Gaines says of the collection, "[O]nce I realized that I was writing a group of stories that had some similarities, I wanted them to have relationship with the other ones." He cites that relationship as being one of "progression," in which "'A Long Day in November' is like planting a grain, and it's sprouting" (Ingram and Steinberg, 342). Moving through each story in the collection are many progressions, from boyhood to manhood, innocence to awareness, isolation to fellowship, past to present, life to death. By making the central character of the final story a female, there is even a progression from the gender-specific "arrival to manhood" theme to a more encompassing universal theme of spiritual arrival.

The transformations within *Bloodline* give the collection a feeling of growth. All the characters are on the brink of change, and they quest for the resolve and courage to make this change a positive step toward self-awareness. The movement of diverse characters becomes unified as all set out on odysseys that promise to transform their self-conceptions. Gaines takes very basic human experiences—Sonny's wetting himself, James's toothache, Proctor's involvement in a barroom brawl—and unites them into a common story of life as a journey with obstacles and potential rewards. Characters are tried by forces within themselves and the forces of society, but they endure, and the emergence of a dignified self able to triumph over any obstacle becomes a fundamental experience in this collection and Gaines's subsequent fiction.

A crucial element in all the quests collected here is the realization of the role of family and community in the formation of identity. Sonny and James are young enough to still be in contact with their family, but Eddie, Proctor, and Copper must respectively reunite, re-create, and reclaim family to make it part of their identities. Knowing the place of self within the community is equally important, even when the community becomes increasingly threatening as the stories move from the safety of Sonny's quarters, through the segregated environment James traverses, to the menacing prison environment of Proctor, and to the hostile society that coaxes Copper into madness. However perilous the environs, only when communal and familial identity are combined can a full self be realized, as is symbolically represented in the final story, in which many personalities join to produce an extended community's identity.

While there is a sense of progression among the stories, there is also a sense of cycle that gives the collection a feeling of constant renewal. "Just Like a Tree" is both a return to the old and a resurrection of the new: as Fe dies, the values of dignity and self-worth that she stood for live on in Emmanuel, who carries on her fight in another generation. These values also live on in subsequent Gaines fiction, whether actually personified in a descendant of Aunt Fe, Jane Pittman, or used as the goals for which such characters as Marcus in *Of Love and Dust* and the old men in *A Gathering of Old Men* are willing to sacrifice their lives. Though many of his characters will fail in their quest for respect, though some are defeated before they begin, they each share the potential for significant transformation and the capacity to attempt to change themselves and their world for the better.

Chapter Three

Et in Arcadia Ego: The Declining Pastoral of *Catherine Carmier*

To smell that Louisiana earth, feel that Louisiana sun.

—Ernest Gaines

Rural Louisiana seems to inspire literary tributes. George Washington Cable was one of the first nineteenth-century writers to create a fiction immersed in it, and Kate Chopin continued the legacy, making Creole manners a key element in her fiction.[1] It influences all of Ernest Gaines's works, but nowhere is its presence more strongly felt than in his first published novel, *Catherine Carmier*.[2] The novel intertwines natural elements with the sensibilities of characters to weave a pastoral of love, land, and racial pride.

The definitions of pastoral are many. In its most basic sense a pastoral represents the contrast of a simpler mode of life with a more complex one. In another sense it can be seen as a retreat from ordinary life to an idyllic setting that fosters a stronger perspective on life in a complex world. In still another sense it can signify the contrast between the beauty of God's Eden and the corruption of man's earth. All these implications are present in *Catherine Carmier*. The work is set in the beauty of rural Louisiana, where racial and social relations have remained relatively unchanged since the time of slavery. Unchanging relations lend an aura of stability to the novel's community, and the work exhibits the pastoral's essential withdrawal from modern confusions to a simpler place apart. The central character descends from the introspective shepherds, hunters, poets, children, or dethroned kings that people pastorals and give perspectives on what humankind has done to itself and nature.

In keeping with the pastoral tradition, characters in *Catherine Carmier* comprehend life through nature. Night to day, fertility to drought, winter to spring become their points of reference as they attempt to understand the freedom and enclosure that form the polarities of their lives. Rural Louisi-

45

ana is both a backdrop for their story and an integral part of their psyche. Who they are and what motivates them are intricately tied to the land that has nurtured them, as they observe the passage of time and its mutations. *Catherine Carmier* is a pastoral, but one in decline. Romantic love is destroyed by anachronistic race and caste values, and land and a way of life are destroyed by a changing epoch.

Somewhat reminiscent of Shakespeare's *Romeo and Juliet*, the novel relates the story of the ill-fated love shared by Jackson Bradley and Catherine Carmier. As a boy, Jackson grew up in a parish modeled after Gaines's native community. He has been sent north for further education, and returns to a world that is now alien to him. His education has distanced him from the very people who ordained him leader and teacher when they sent him north, and Jackson has become an outsider. His homecoming sets the contrast characteristic of the pastoral in motion. He must reassess the accepted values of the parish in terms of those he has acquired in San Francisco; he must reconcile past idyll with present reality. In a manner that will characterize psychological portraits throughout the novel, Jackson's estrangement from his community is conveyed through comparisons he makes between his condition and the landscape's.

Jackson's Louisiana "Arcadia," a rural world of beauty and imperceptible social change, is gone, in part because Cajuns are gradually overtaking the land. In the early 1600s French peasant settlers came to the New World to participate in a growing trade of fur and native American goods and created Acadia in present-day Nova Scotia. The mid-1700s saw an English colonial government, made increasingly Francophobic by the onset of the French and Indian War, force the Acadians out of Nova Scotia and give them the option of resettling in any French territory. Some migrated to the French West Indies; others returned to France; and from 1757 to 1770, with assistance from the French and Spanish governments, approximately 1,000 migrated to Louisiana in hope of creating what they called the New Acadia.[3]

Initially the Acadians settled in rural prairies along the Vermilion and Atchafalaya rivers, areas distant from the existing plantations of the European-born colonial elite. The end of slavery, the advent of sharecropping, epidemic disease, scarcity of fertile land, and a growing population set another migratory wave in motion, and Acadians, now popularly referred to as Cajuns,[4] began sharecropping the land black slaves and their descendants had worked for generations. This is the legacy Jackson now witnesses upon his return to Louisiana.

The deeding of black farming plots to Cajun farmers has rendered the region once so familiar to Jackson unrecognizable. As he looks at the area he once called home, "[H]e hardly recognized the old place anymore. The old houses that had once stood back there had been torn down. Many of the trees had been cut down and sold for lumber and firewood, and the places where he used to pick pecans and blackberries were now plowed under. Patches of corn, cotton, and sugar cane had taken the place of everything."[5] The reality of economic agrarianism replaces the pastoral ideal, and the felling of trees and the appearance of commodity crops are physical changes complementing Jackson's alienation from his community and past. The only remaining tie to his previous existence is his love for the Creole Catherine. Catherine's father, Raoul, however, steeped in the rigid and archaic color code of Creole society, forbids Catherine to love Jackson because he is black, and jealously demands that he, and no other man, be the center of his favorite daughter's affection. A direct contrast to Jackson, who no longer has bonds to the past, Raoul has no ties to the future and lives in his own sphere of outmoded creeds rooted in the Creole caste system of New Orleans.

The term *Creole* is a complex one, and the difficulty in defining it mirrors Raoul's difficulty in defining himself. *Creole* has been used as a classifier of many things, from race to culture, from language to cuisine. It has variously referred to diverse social, political, cultural, and economic groups as well. In Louisiana it has denoted whites of Spanish, French, or Italian descent who settled in Louisiana, as well as the descendants of European slaveholders and African slaves who upon manumission were known as *gens de couleur libre*, free people of color. As the term is used in *Catherine Carmier*, it refers to the latter group, who emerged as a third class within a three-tiered society of free persons, free persons of color, and slaves. It should be noted that while cross-racial interaction might have originally produced the Creole of color class, by the time of the action in *Catherine Carmier* the class was maintained through established intermarriage and distinguished itself even from blacks of biracial heritage. Neither black nor white, the Creoles of color in New Orleans enjoyed a distinct racial and class status and flourished economically and socially under both French and Spanish rule of Louisiana. Even in the slavery era they had rights similar to those of white citizens, though they could not intermarry with or receive legal legacies from whites. Such a cloistered society developed a strict social code to guarantee its insularity.[6]

This unique history of racial and ethnic separatism engulfs Raoul Carmier. He is bound to the codes of his Creole social order, and his inflexible adherence to its segregationist philosophy separates him from the other black farmers of his parish. He thus has no allies to assist him in fending off the encroaching Cajun presence, whose clannishness and technology allow them to cultivate more land more efficiently. His only companion is his land, and to it he retreats from the complexities of changing race relations. Refusing to suffer the simultaneous loss of his land to the Cajuns and his daughter to Jackson, Raoul crusades to keep Catherine and Jackson apart. As with Jackson, every mutation in Raoul's psychological state is manifested through images taken from the land; indeed, Raoul and his land are indistinguishable.

The nature images that accompany each character's struggle to understand change convey the importance of land to the psyche of a rural people while at the same time illustrate the manner in which a landscape made unrecognizable by new technology forces them to confront ongoing displacements. No character is left untouched by change, and the following conversation between Brother, one of the few remaining black farmers, and a group of Cajun farmers subtly foreshadows the loss of traditions that occurs when one ethnic group replaces another and a new technology replaces an old one:

"Taking the day off, huh?"

"Waiting for that tractor," the other Cajun said.

"Y'all getting another one?" Brother asked.

"Yeah. Everybody got one now."

"Reckon'd you can destroy some land with all of 'em going," Brother said. (CC, 6)

On one level Brother's use of the word *destroy* is simply a colloquialism, but on another it implies bitterness toward the Cajuns who take not only land but also what the black farmers see as birthrights. For black farmers the land gives sustenance, but it is also the only legacy they can leave to future generations. As they raze the land, the Cajuns also raze African-American familial continuity, leaving the black farmers nothing but reflections on their loss:

"Wouldn't 'a' thought ten years ago the Cajuns would 'a' been running things now. . . ."

"It been coming," someone else said.

"It ain't just coming. It here now," the young man said. "The only thing you can do is get away. . . ." The men . . . were silent—reflecting the fate the Cajuns and their machines had bestowed upon them and their children. (CC, 61–62)

The fate of the land is the fate of the black farmers, as they too are hewn, left with no landscape by which to define themselves. They join the other characters within the work who, when confronted with no longer belonging, contemplate the land and remember a simpler time.

Pastoral imagery illuminates each character's reaction to a world of changing axioms. The homecoming of Catherine's sister, Lillian, is another instance. Raoul has sent Lillian to his sisters in Baton Rouge, ostensibly to be reared "as a lady" but more importantly to be reared as a Creole. The result of Lillian's education is a displacement similar to the one Jackson, Raoul, and the black farmers experience. She no longer feels at home in the black community, and because of her status as a Creole of color, is not completely accepted into the white world whose etiquette she has adopted. As she tells her sister, Catherine, "I hate black. . . . I haven't opened my heart out to that white world either. But I'm going there because I must go somewhere. I can't stand in the middle of the road any longer" (*CC*, 48). Lillian is driven to contemplate "passing" (masquerading as white) because the values that created a distinct Creole class no longer have meaning in her present existence. Her proposed plan of action only portends further alienation, and a quotation from Virginia R. Dominguez's *White by Definition* illustrates why:

Dichotomization forces those who try to pass to maintain absolutely no contact with the family and the friends they leave behind. Any such contact could arouse suspicion, and with suspicion comes demotion and a return to "colored" status.

The successful *passablanc* [one passing for white] breeds both jealousy and pride in the community he leaves behind. It is a situation to which many have reluctantly resigned themselves. They fault not the individuals who pass but the dichotomous system of classification that forces them to pass. Hence, many colored Creoles protect others who are trying to pass, to the point of feigning ignorance of certain branches of their families. Elicited genealogies often seem strangely skewed. . . . [O]ne very good informant . . . confided in me that his own mother's sister and her children had passed into the white community. With tears in his eyes, he described the painful experience of learning about his aunt's death on the obituary page of the *New Orleans Times Picayune*. His cousins failed to inform the abandoned side of the family of the death, for fear that they might show up at the wake or the funeral and thereby destroy the image of whiteness. Total separation was necessary for secrecy.[7]

Lillian opts for the isolation and total separation Dominguez describes, rather than the ambivalent state of existing between two races. As she gropes for place, she too retreats to the natural landscape around her to make sense of a world that provides her with no clear self-definition. While driving back from the railroad station, she looks out on the river, recalls a less complex time, and voices to Catherine her resentment of the social power whites wield:

"The idle rich," she said. "The idle white rich. Do they still fish out there?"
  "Some," Catherine said. "But they use it mostly now for racing—stuff like that."
  "They won't even let the poor fish in peace," Lillian said. . . . "We must always remember it's theirs to do what they want with it." (*CC*, 39)

Lillian's comment "We must always remember it's theirs to do what they want with it" alludes to both the landscape and her own powerlessness within a white world. Her bitterness toward the "idle white rich" who while pursuing their recreational interests "won't even let the poor fish in peace" is a projection of her bitterness toward a society that she believes pursues its own interests in demarcating race and caste with indifferent disregard for the casualties of this demarcation, such as herself. Like the other characters in this work, Lillian finds refuge in a memory of nature as she faces the erosion of her existing worldview. Her subsequent actions represent a pattern that is repeated for each major character in the novel: a character encounters change, then seeks refuge in a communion with nature or the memory of unspoiled nature.

  While conventions of the pastoral inform the treatment of characters and nature, another literary influence is also evident in the handling of their response to change: that of Ivan Turgenev. Gaines has the following to say on the effect reading Turgenev has had on his writing:

I discovered Turgenev's *A Sportsman's Sketches*. That was about hunting and meeting people in rural life. And then, the clarity and the beauty of his writing, even in translation. Then I discovered *Fathers and Sons*. It was a simple, small book. . . . And this small book had just about everything that a small book can have. And, too, at the time I discovered Turgenev I could almost see myself in Bazarov's position, you know? When you go back, *what*? Not that I'd become a nihilist, but I could understand the nihilistic attitude after someone had been away awhile. . . . My *Catherine Carmier* is almost written on the structure of *Fathers and Sons*. As a matter of fact, that was my Bible.[8]

One of the clearest parallels between *Catherine Carmier* and *Fathers and Sons* is the similarity between Jackson and Bazarov.

  During a vacation from school Bazarov returns to the country from St.

Petersburg, and the education he acquired in the city collides with the people and traditions of the village. He advocates nihilism and rejects religion and the class system of his time. Wanting to change society but having no clear plan as to how to accomplish such change, he transfers his frustration onto the people of the community to whom he was once tied, resenting what he sees as their ignorance, superstition, and acquiescence to the ruling class. Jackson's education, like Bazarov's, makes homecoming difficult, and, very much removed from his southern community, Jackson regards it with the cold eye of an indifferent analyst. The ideals he left home with are replaced with cynicism, as he realizes the promise of the North is "all a pile of lies": "They don't come dressed in white sheets with ropes. But there's no truth" (*CC*, 81). Jackson's schooling enables him to discern the blatant injustice done to the black farmers of his community and what appears to be their complacent acceptance of a race and caste hierarchy that relegates them to servitude. The one observation fills him with anger; the other, with hopelessness. His frustration becomes acute when he observes an even more deleterious form of racism, the self-hatred at the root of the Creole values that separate him from Catherine.

Jackson's questioning traps him between the tensions of his past world and those of his present, between finding no place in the North and remaining a stranger in his native South. His alienation is represented through the increasing distance between him and the aunt who reared him, Charlotte. Like those devout, kindhearted, ancient provincials, father and mother Bazarov, Charlotte is an aged woman who believes in sacrificing all for the betterment of the next generation. Her constant, selfless giving stifles Jackson, but his affection for her renders him incapable of telling her he can no longer carry the burden of her pride or her hopes. The most telling juncture in their relationship comes with the revelation that Jackson cannot accept the God and religion so essential to Charlotte's faith and daily coping. He terms her Christ and her church a "bourgeois farce," and the two-dimensionality he perceives in her devotion is represented through the faded image of Christ on a four-year-old calendar given her by one peddling more secular forms of secured deliverance, an insurance agent.

The growing discomfort Jackson feels as he returns from the North and reflects on his dying relationship with Charlotte, her religion, and his community causes him to retreat into a contemplation of nature, and his displacement is represented through images of deadened nature as he looks out on his aunt's declining garden:

Jackson stood by the window, looking into the garden. The half-dozen rows of beans that ran beside the house were nearly dry. Everything else in the garden had that half-green, half-yellow color. . . .

I should have told her, he was thinking. I should have told her then that I'm going back. How can anyone stay here? Just look at this place. Everything is drying up; everything is half dead.

Am I any better off? Am I any more alive than either one of these hills of beans—accusing an old woman for wrecking this wretched life, and the only sin she ever committed was loving me? . . . I'm in the same class. . . dry, dead. (*CC*, 102)

In the barrenness of the surrounding land, Jackson finds symbolic empathy for his withering familial and communal ties. As his relationship to his community deteriorates, a divide appears between its values and his, and once Jackson initiates an involvement with Catherine, eradicating that division becomes impossible.

Resenting the Creoles for what they feel is a supercilious disdain, the blacks of Jackson's quarters do not approve of one of their own entering into a liaison with one whose culture rejects theirs. Their disavowal of him increases his alienation, and his observations of nature render the isolation enveloping him. Images of darkness, of curtains being drawn, pervade many of his descriptions, as is seen in the following passage: "He looked at the old cypress tree down the riverbank. Gray-black Spanish moss hung from every limb like long, ugly curtains. Jackson felt as though these curtains hung over his heart" (*CC*, 173). Although Jackson attempts to open the curtains that emotionally isolate him, he cannot, and seeks Catherine as "his light," a beacon illuminating a possible path of escape from his confinement. Ironically, however, his love for her roots him in the very land he wants to be free of and ties him to the very past he wants to flee.

When Jackson no longer can make sense of conflicting desires, he confides in his former teacher Madame Bayonne.[9] As he confesses his confusion to her, as well as his desire to escape, he temporarily superimposes his consciousness on an owl in flight:

"I'm not looking for a paradise, Madame Bayonne.". . .

She looked at him, but did not answer.

An owl suddenly left an old pecan tree about a hundred yards from where Jackson and Madame Bayonne were standing, and went flying over the field and across the road. The owl flew so low over their heads that Jackson could almost hear the beating of its wings. He watched it fly over the house and into the night. He wondered what had caused it to leave and where it would eventually stop. (*CC*, 81–82)

Jackson's uncertainty of the owl's origin and ultimate destination reflects his uncertainty about his own situation. He longs to take flight, but having no direction to follow, flits from one state of restlessness to another. Jackson tells Madame Bayonne, "I'm like a leaf . . . that's broken away from the tree. Drifting" (*CC*, 79). Every element of the natural world around him, from the owl to the dust to the leaves, seems empathetic to his uneasiness and the uneasiness felt by the woman he loves, Catherine.

Like Jackson, Catherine is torn between her own desires and the values of her father and family. She has grown up in the quarters, but unlike Jackson, has had no opportunity for escape, and actually no desire. Her first tenuous foray into independence, through a union with the father of her child, another Creole farmer, met with obdurate resistance from Raoul and reconciled Catherine to surveying her father's farm as her universe. Though no incest is implied, she usurps her mother's place as Raoul's wife. Connected so deeply to her family and their homestead, she personifies the Louisiana land and her love becomes a pastoral retreat for Jackson.

The regularity of Catherine's life with Raoul is like the regularity of the seasons, but it is upset when Jackson returns. As her determination to love Jackson increases, her relationship with her father begins to parallel Jackson's and Charlotte's struggles to reconcile past and future. Jackson is the confrontation with change that will trigger Catherine's seeking refuge in images of the landscape so familiar to her, and impressionistic descriptions of nature are interspersed among her reflections on the various phases of their relationship. When, for example, she must decide whether to leave the familiarity of her world to enter the uncertainty of the world Jackson promises, her feelings for him, Raoul, and the land collide. Her thoughts fragment into remembered moments with Raoul and images of the physical landscape:

She had no control over anything any more—neither her mind, nor her heart. Ideas came into her mind, but went out just as fast. She caught glimpses of trees, . . . the river, but the next moment all of it had slipped by. She sat there as though she were paralyzed—not being able to think properly, nor being able to move. I will not see Bayonne again, I will not see the trees again, I will not see the river again, I will not see him, my father, again. . . . Will she ever see this again? The Grovers' big house? the store? the cypress trees? the riverbank? the river? Will she ever see it black and lonely like this again? (*CC*, 231–33)

As much as she is pained by the prospect of being torn from her father and family, Catherine is pained by the prospect of being torn from the land and its traditions. The isolation she foresees is represented in the image of the river, "black and lonely," and her final decision is also rendered in a statement that shows how closely related nature, family, and self are in Catherine's psyche: "I love them. No, I love him. . . . Before he came I loved them. No, I've always loved him, and I always will. . . . What will he think if I tell him it is not right to go— . . . I must stay. . . . I . . . the trees go by, the houses go by, the cars, the fences, the river, Louisiana—my life" (*CC*, 232). Unlike Jackson, Catherine has a secure sense of place. In the physical and social landscape of the quarters, she has the belonging that Jackson will continue to seek until he can reconcile his past with his present. The peace she finds at home is more valuable to her than the illusive freedom he represents, and she elects the concrete meaning of her world over the abstract emptiness of his.

Severing Catherine from her community is akin to rendering an element of nature from its habitat, and the void that would be left is reminiscent of the one felt by Fe's community in "Just Like a Tree." Though her presence isn't as vital to the entire community as Fe's is to hers, Catherine's nearness is vital to the one character who intervenes to prevent her exodus with Jackson, her father. For Raoul to let go of Catherine is to let go of all that has any significance for him. He is fighting to preserve his identity as a Creole of color, to retain his land against an inevitable Cajun encroachment, and he cannot face the prospect of losing another element crucial to his psychological survival. In a world that is changing faster than Raoul can acknowledge, Catherine remains his only constant.

Raoul's obsession with land and color has not only isolated him from his community but also fragmented his family. Lillian can no longer abide the strict Creole color code that is essential to his identity and tells Catherine, "Daddy and his sisters can't understand this. They want us to be Creoles. Creoles. What a joke. Today you're one way or the other; you're white or you're black. There is no in-between" (*CC*, 48). He is estranged from his wife Della because jealousy drives him to kill Mark Carmier, her son by a black sharecropper, ostensibly in an accident while chopping cane. In Raoul's subsequent reflections on the incident, what becomes quietly clear is that both Della's infidelity and her choice of lover, a *black* sharecropper, fuel his hatred of Mark.[10] As he contemplates Catherine and Jackson's relationship, he sees her as repeating her mother's transgression by breaking the same color taboo. In his mind he fuses past and present, his hatred of Jackson and his hatred of blackness, his suppressed love for Mark and his memory of Della's infidelity, and the following confused mixture of emotions is the result:

He will have his black arms around her waist. He will have his black mouth on her red lips. . . . I will raise the gun. I will—he started thinking about the other boy. It was like a song that you could not get out of your mind. It was like your skin that you must live inside of forever. (Contrary to what the others believed, he loved the boy. Ten thousand times he had wanted to pull the boy to him . . . to whisper "I love you," but something always kept him from doing so. . . . "Hate him," the thing was saying to him. Look what she's done. Hate him. Hate him." And all the time he wanted to love the boy.) (*CC*, 228)

Pride prohibits Raoul from reaching out to Mark, and he loses a boy that might have been a son. His firm adherence to the Creole code forbids his reaching out to the other black farmers, and he loses potential allies in his fight to keep the land that means so much to him. His self-imposed seclusion imbues him with a power that seems to border on madness, and he is obsessed with futilely fighting change, consumed by battling the machines of the Cajuns.

Raoul's animosity toward the Cajuns has historical antecedents. In describing to Jackson the causes for Raoul's isolation, Madame Bayonne with "eyes that know everything" (*CC*, 70), summarizes the history of black and Cajun relationships that is a cornerstone in Gaines's work:

White is still white, Jackson. . . . and white still sticks with white. . . . The Cajuns have always made more crop . . . than the Negroes have. They've always had the best land—being white they got that from the start; and they have organization. . . . Having the best land and being able to work it all together, they grew twice as much. When you make twice as much, you can afford to buy more equipment. Once they got the equipment, they wanted more land to work. So Bud Grover gave them the land—acre by acre until the Negro's farm was too small to support him. He quits, and the Cajuns get it all. . . . Now, they've all quit. All but one. (*CC*, 73–74)

This explanation and other similar conversations illustrate Gaines's use of dialogue to insert topics of social interest into his novels. *Catherine Carmier* fuses characters' visions and political issues, and social commentary dramatizes personal conflict. The result is a combining of the politics of white, Cajun, Creole, and black with a romantic love story.

A subsequent conversation between Jackson and Madame Bayonne further exemplifies the inlaying of politics into the novel's dialogues. As she articulates why the land is so essential to both Raoul's physical and psychological existence, Madame Bayonne describes how land connects

Raoul to his Creole ancestry and the function of the Creole class in a society
based on race and caste distinction:

> [T]hough he was as white as any white man, he still had a drop of Negro blood in
> him, and because of that single drop of blood, it would be impossible to ever com-
> pete side by side with the white man. So he went to the land—away from the white
> man, away from the black man as well . . . where he would not have to
> compete—at least side by side—with either. . . . His love for his land, his hatred
> for the white man, the contempt with which he looks upon the black man has
> passed from one generation to the other.
>   Raoul did not choose his position. . . . He is only carrying out something that
> was cut out for him in the beginning. He has no control over it. . . . He was put
> there by the white man and the black man alike. The white man will not let Raoul
> compete with him because of that drop of Negro blood, and at the same time he
> has put the Negro in such a position that Raoul would rather die than compete
> with him. (*CC*, 116–17)

Raoul's position and, by extension, the position of the Creole class reveal
the manipulation of racial hostilities to ensure that power continues to rest
in the hands of a white ruling class. Placed as a buffer between the black
race and the white, Creole disdain for blacks ensured a tacit assistance in
black downgrading and afforded whites a measure of ease.

Unable to separate his belief in his Creole aristocracy from his reverence
for his land, Raoul, seeing the values of his culture eroding, clings tightly to
the land and even more tightly to the one person he feels understands what
it means to him, Catherine. She and the land share equally in his affection
and at points in his consciousness become analogous. In his esteem
Catherine is different from his other children. Unlike Mark, she is not a
painful reminder of Della's infidelity; unlike Lillian, she was born before
Raoul's feeling for Della became loathing and is not subjected to the guilt
by association he imposes upon his second daughter. The teachings of his
great-grandfather, grandfather, and father have historically prepared him for
the likely loss of his land to the Cajuns, but nothing has prepared him for
the loss of Catherine. While the Cajuns are an enemy Raoul can understand, Jackson is not.

The realization that Catherine could love another man besides himself,
particularly a black man, jars Raoul's conception of the world and threatens
to destroy it. Like Lillian, Jackson, and Catherine, he must now confront the
change he has been denying, and in doing so, his reflections meander between thoughts of Catherine and thoughts of his land: "Catherine would
never . . . he knew she was lonely. Of course she was lonely. A girl at that

age . . . No, no, no, he was wrong. He was imagining this, because those niggers had told him that about her. He did not believe them. They were doing this to hurt him. The Cajuns were probably behind it all. They wanted his land. He knew it. They would do anything to hurt him, to make him pack up and leave. They would . . . he wondered if she would do this to him" (*CC*, 226–27). The mixture of references to both Catherine and his farm shows the two to be indistinguishable in Raoul's confused mind, and aborting her involvement with Jackson becomes his second obsession. The final scene of the novel is a confrontation between Raoul and Jackson, but in a larger sense it is the culminating confrontation between all the oppositions Gaines creates in the rest of the novel: past versus future, black versus Cajun, black versus Creole.

In challenging Jackson, Raoul seeks to purge himself of tormenting change. Throughout the fight he superimposes Mark's aspect on Jackson's, and while fighting him he is simultaneously fighting both blackness and infidelity. Just as he tried to eradicate the painful memory Mark embodied, so does he try to eradicate the threatening future Jackson forebodes. His favorite daughter desires a life with a black man, and battling Jackson is his final attempt to deny the realization that the rigid Creole values he has lived by are no longer appropriate. Further, the daughter so synonymous with his farm chooses to love a man other than himself, and his contest with Jackson additionally represents a final endeavor to retain the symbol of his land. The confluence of past and present, real and symbolic overwhelms Raoul, and he is left unsure, bewildered, and despondent: "His eyes were on Jackson, who stood before him. He did not look at him angrily. Instead, he seemed puzzled. He tried to grasp what was happening to him. He would not believe that he was beaten. There was too much left for him to do. There was the crop to get in; there was Catherine. How could he possibly fall? What would become of everything if he did?" (*CC*, 241). As Raoul contemplates his defeat, he again does not distinguish between the loss of Catherine, the loss of his land, and the loss of his social conceptions, as implied through his questioning, "[W]hat would become of *everything*?" Images of nature represent his vain attempts to hold on to his identity in the face of inescapable change. His land becomes his escape from social reality, giving him everything he needs for existence, and not demanding that he submit to the complexities of modern identification.

Nature provides refuge to Raoul and also to other characters confronting change and its psychic impact. The swamps, for example, the lesser land relegated to black farmers because of their poor potential, become terra firma for black characters. They provide an insular retreat within the quarters, keeping the manipulations of the white ruling class and the encroaching presence of the Cajuns at bay. In another instance, Madame Bayonne's bushes shield her yard from the outside world, and by a metaphorical extension protect her from the temporal changes occurring in the community: "She went into the yard, and the tall flower bushes and the trees in the yard seemed to envelop her, hiding her from him in the road. Or did these things hide the road, the outside from her?" (*CC*, 82). Similarly, the Carmier house is surrounded by "[T]he big oak and pecan trees," which, "like sentinels" (*CC*, 190), form a barrier between them and the rest of the quarters. Nature silently guards the community from the exigencies of change. Ever watchful, it conceals the passage of time and allows all to live in the shadows of a simpler but decaying past. But as the trees are felled and the land cultivated, the dense protection nature provides disappears, and the community must face the onset of new values.

Catherine Carmier becomes what Harold E. Toliver terms an "antipastoral," a work of "pastoral failure" that describes "an inability to stay inside the protected world."[11] Encroaching change pushes the characters out of their Louisiana Arcadia and compels them to confront personal, racial, and temporal truths. As past and future collide, the old people so intertwined with the landscape that "[T]hey were like trees, like rocks, like the ocean" (*CC*, 171) are replaced by the younger Jacksons and Lillians whose rootlessness contrasts sharply with the rootedness of their elders. The quarters, cloistered from change since Reconstruction, now face the extinction of a way of life. Though there has been inequity, there has also been continuity, and the community has had a sense of an unchanging identity. The constancy it has experienced in the past is eroding, however; its young people have departed and once its older members die, so will traditions and customs. Because *Catherine Carmier* captures this disappearing community in such detail, the novel itself becomes a refuge from change.

Through realistic characters and photographic images *Catherine Carmier* enshrines the life and traditions of a particular Louisiana parish. One of the novel's most successful memorials to this community in transition lies in its incorporation of the oral tradition that has passed on its history. The language of *Catherine Carmier* rings with the cadences of living storytellers. In Viney's speech, for example, we hear the cadences of black dialect: "Well, he done met just about everybody. . . . And I recon'd I'm go'n be heading on home" (*CC*, 67); Francois's speech echoes Cajun inflections: "Yeah, I hear 'em talk 'bout him there. . . . So he come visit the people, hanh? . . . And what he do here?" (*CC*, 5); and the narrative structure of the novel reproduces the orality of this community.

Though *Catherine Carmier* is related in the third person, often the omniscient narrator conspicuously turns the telling of the story over to a character. The overall effect is to evoke an interchange between speaker and listener rather than text and reader:

> One summer afternoon, Robert Carmier rode up to the plantation store (the store was still being managed by the Grovers then) and asked Mack Grover for the house. (Antoine Richard, who was at the store, brought this version of the story to the quarters.) "What color are you?" Mack Grover wanted to know. "I'm a colored man," Robert Carmier said, "but I can farm as well as the next one." Mack Grover told him that he had a smaller house farther down the quarters that he would let him have. Robert Carmier repeated that he could farm as well as any man and better than most. . . .
> Antoine Richard said there was silence after this, and he lowered his head to look at the floor. (*CC*, 8–9)

The account of the homecoming party given in Jackson's honor is another example of the orality permeating the narrative voice of the text: "Brother, who was in charge of seeing that everything went all right, was all over the place. First you saw him in the kitchen, then the living room, then out on the porch, and finally in the yard. . . . Whenever he came into the kitchen, he got himself a bottle of beer out of the washtub near the door, uncapped the bottle on an opener on the wall, and stood there a moment drinking and looking around" (*CC*, 59). The informality of the third-person voice, combined with the tacit implication of the reader as a listener through use of the phrase "First you saw," encourages a conversational relationship between the reader and the narrator that gives the illusion of a storyteller passing on information.

The tone of the novel modulates depending on which character reveals information, and the customary dialogue is replaced throughout with indirect discourse, as in this passage, in which an implied storyteller takes center stage: "When Selina got ready to leave, she told them that the only thing troubling Charlotte was that she needed rest. Mary Louise said that she would stay there the remainder of the night. Selina said it was not necessary since Charlotte was already asleep. Mary Louise insisted that she would stay. Selina said that she would be back tomorrow morning and she told everyone goodnight. Brother and Mary Louise told her good night, and Mary Louise went inside to sit by the bed" (*CC*, 165–66). The narrative voice here and elsewhere in *Catherine Carmier* may derive from the world of storytellers Gaines recalls from his youth:

I come from a plantation, where people told stories by the fireplace at night, people told stories on the ditch bank. . . . People sat around telling stories. I think in my immediate family there were tremendous storytellers or liars or whatever you want to call them. . . . Say there was a funeral today, or a wedding, the old people would sort of gather in a little room and they would talk about things. . . . They might start with the wedding, or they might start with that particular funeral, but by the time they end up, they've talked about everything that happened in the last twenty years. (Laney, 3)

The oral quality of *Catherine Carmier* will develop into the bond joining all Gaines's novels. Even at this early point in his career, the two characteristic traits of his fiction are evident: the remembering of a special place and the rendering of its oral discourse.

Catherine Carmier is Gaines's first full-length tribute to his rural parish. Its germ was the novel he penned at 16 when he was desperate for the feel of Louisiana in his new California home, and remnants of his displacement are seen in the change affecting his characters and their community. His memory of its landscape becomes the images of nature that document the inevitability of change, and the work is his pastoral contrasting the lonely complexity of his life in San Francisco to the nostalgic simplicity of rural Louisiana.

Even in Pointe Coupée, however, change and its accompanying intricacies were inevitable, and *Et in Arcadia ego* ("Death is even in Arcadia") becomes a fitting motto for the dying idyll of *Catherine Carmier.*[12] The stability of the community lends the illusion of a contented peace, but change menaces this peace just as death menaces the eternal happiness of Arcady. Increasing tensions among the various cultural groups of the parish, a need for new values to deal with a new society, and the many physical changes affecting the land are the harbingers of a complex modernity that signals the demise of simplicity. Besides being a novel of character and event, *Catherine Carmier* is a novel of place, recalling a time now past but accessible through memory and captured in a unique literature.

Chapter Four
Fighting the Odds in
Of Love and Dust

If you stay out the graveyard nigger, I'll keep you out the pen.
—Lightin' Hopkins, "Mr. Tim Moore's Farm"

The opportunities available to a black man in rural Louisiana of the 1940s and 1950s were few. As the Lightin' Hopkins blues verse just quoted popularly generalizes, those opportunities were often limited to death or jail. Inspired by the sentiments of this blues ballad, Gaines, in his second published novel, *Of Love and Dust,* explores the narrow orbit of possibilities afforded a black man in a racist environment.[1] The determinism of the novel's milieu forebodes inevitable tragedy, and the work is often suggestive of the manner in which the Greek masters treated tragedy. The hero, Marcus Payne, possesses a tragic flaw that leads him to believe he can beat the odds of the bigoted system that governs him. He attempts to trick his fate by controlling his destiny, and tragically, he pays for his hubris with his life. His actions are closely bound to the destinies of others and ultimately will have a dire impact on those close to him.[2]

The tragedy of *Of Love and Dust* unfolds in an environment now familiar to Gaines readers. We are reacquainted with the world of the quarters, of the plantation, and we are reintroduced to two familiar Gaines themes, Cajun encroachment and the devaluation of black life. The description of land distribution in which "[t]he Cajuns had the front-est and best land, and the colored people (those who were still hanging on) had the middle and worst land,"[3] recalls the unfair land distribution and displacement found in "Just Like a Tree" and *Catherine Carmier.* The account of the fight in which Marcus kills a man is reminiscent of Proctor Lewis's obvious disregard of black humanity in "Three Men." *Of Love and Dust* echoes earlier Gaines fiction while describing a young man's attempt to defy destiny and rule his own life.

The novel's technique also provides a sense of continuity between works through its simulation of oral storytelling in writing. The narrator who reveals Marcus's story is 33-year-old James Kelly, a field-worker who personifies an oral storyteller. He gets along with all on the plantation, black and white, and has carved a comfortable niche of complacency for himself within the plantation system. In the words of John Edgar Wideman, Jim is "both an individual and a chorus. Like the chorus of Greek tragedy he has the privilege of near omniscience, of the wisdom, experience and critical acuity of the entire community. He can float disembodied like the chorus into other characters' minds, revealing their innermost thoughts and feelings."[4] Wideman's likening of Jim to the chorus of a Greek tragedy is an appropriate and important allusion. While Jim narrates the story, he often speaks for the community, representing its traditional moral, religious, and social attitudes. His role in the novel underscores a significant likeness between the social order depicted in Greek tragedy and the order here: that both are governed by strict rules, and their maintenance depends upon adherence to these rules. When one character steps outside the boundaries of society's precepts, as does Marcus, the result is havoc within the entire system.

As a choral character, Jim provides a communal perspective by which to judge Marcus's actions.[5] His popularity throughout the quarters conveys a communal acceptance that makes him a narrator with a comprehensive vision of the parish whose annals he reports. As in the following passage, he often tells a story within a story, digressing to give ample information about the environment and motivations influencing his subjects:

But wait, wait, I'm getting a little ahead of myself. I jumped to the weekend when I should have stopped at Thursday—because Thursday at twelve o'clock, Marcus saw Pauline Guerin for the first time. He was riding on the tractor beside me. . . . He was telling me about the boy he had killed. He said it was over a woman. It happened at a nightclub. The nightclub was packed and hot. There were women everywhere—women, women, and more women. . . . Oh yes, he said, he had forgot to tell me he had been gambling all evening and had won a pile of money. (*LD*, 52)

What is important to the present action of the novel is that Marcus is seeing Pauline for the first time, but the imbedded nightclub story reveals Marcus's nonchalant attitude toward killing and women, a characteristic that will influence his actions throughout the rest of the novel.

Jim's presence as a storyteller is frequently emphasized in the novel's texture. A variety of Louisiana dialects, from black to white to Cajun, are imbedded in his speech, and the dominance of narrative voice over dialogue first seen in *Catherine Carmier* is continued here as Jim speaks for other characters: "I can't read minds, but if eyes could talk, this is what Marcus and Marshall were saying to each other" (*LD*, 230). He reports incidents in what might be termed a "she said, he said" format, and when absent from an event, he generally identifies an informant who fills the gaps in the narrative action, doing so in the following manner: "Marcus came down the quarter above seven o'clock that night. (I wasn't there, I had gone to Bayonne with Snuke and them to see that woman again. Aunt Margaret told me what time he came home)" (*LD*, 190). Because Jim's perspective is the perspective of a group, the shared tragedy Marcus's actions will bring upon the community is augmented. Jim's comprehensive point of view incorporates characters who anxiously observe actions, await retribution, and know that, as a community, all will be held responsible for the outcome of Marcus's deeds.

Refusing to capitulate to rules that confine him to complacency or subjugation, Marcus fights the odds that limit his options as a black man. He becomes a hero in the tragic sense because he knowingly disregards his society's edicts in the most dangerous fashion he can in the South of the 1940s, by involving himself in miscegenation. Like *Catherine Carmier, Of Love and Dust* is a story of love complicated by race and caste; however, the results of genuine affection across racial lines are much more disastrous in this work.

While awaiting trial for the murder of another black man, Marcus is bonded out of prison. His benefactor is the plantation owner, Marshall Hebert, who has selfish reasons for securing Marcus's release and sends him to his plantation to work off the debt. Immediately upon his arrival Marcus is attracted to Pauline, Hebert's black cook. She, however, is the mistress of the Cajun overseer, Sidney Bonbon, and remains indifferent to Marcus. In revenge, Marcus becomes involved with Louise, Bonbon's white wife, and sets in motion a chain of events that ultimately leads to his death. The complexity of Gaines's plot indicates the complex rigidity of the rules governing black and white interaction in this plantation world. By forming a liaison with Louise, Marcus makes the fatal mistake of living by his own tenets and transgressing the precepts of his society's ideology.

In Marcus's environment, interracial contact is tenaciously regulated. Even simple social acts demand an elaborate decorum, as seen in an instance describing Bonbon and Pauline's day-to-day activities. In order to take Pauline to Baton Rouge so that she can go shopping, Bonbon must use Jim as a cover: "Not that a white man couldn't ride all over the South with a black woman," Jim tells us, but unlike Pauline, who was dressed as any *lady* on a sweltering day might be dressed, in pink with a white straw hat, "the black woman had to look like she was either going to work or coming from work." Jim concludes, "It wouldn't be safe for her to be dressed like Pauline was now. . . . That's why they needed me. She was my wife, not his woman" (*LD*, 140–41). Though somewhat constrained by a racial etiquette that says he must maintain a certain facade, Bonbon, as a white man, still has the freedom to associate publicly with Pauline, and their relationship is tolerated if not accepted. In the parallel relationship in the novel, Marcus and Louise enjoy no such tolerance, and his seduction of Louise becomes an act of rebellion for which only his death can atone.

Every character in the novel acknowledges what must be an obvious and painful truth to Louise, that Sidney Bonbon loved Pauline "more than he did his wife up the quarter or his people who lived on the river" (66). In a sense, by truly loving Pauline he snubs the conventions of the caste system that devalues him as a Cajun along with devaluing blacks. No one verbalizes the truth of Bonbon and Pauline's love, just as no one verbalizes that Pauline's twin sons belong to Bonbon, even "[t]hough every grownup on the place and every child at school knew that Bonbon was Billy and Willy's father" (*LD*, 71). Within this community Bonbon is permitted to exploit Pauline sexually, but not to truly love her, as he does, or acknowledge their children. His society allows him to interact with her in the manner described by Michel Fabre when he states, "The law permits the white man to roll in the hay with any black woman as he would with an animal or a whore precisely because sexuality impedes real sentiment" (Fabre, 116). The same protocol that makes the black woman vulnerable to sexual exploitation also demeans the white woman in this society. Louise Bonbon is kept cloistered, expected to remain chaste and to voice no objection to Sidney's infidelity. For both these women, unions with men across racial lines defy the debased sexist and racist circumstances in which their world has placed them.

Louise and Pauline share a desire to escape the confines of their positions as women. Pauline becomes involved with Bonbon because she is looking for a way out. She realizes the privileges such a relationship can give her, reasoning, "Long as she lived on the plantation she would have to lay with Bonbon. . . . So why not make the best of it? Why not get out of the hot sun? Why not wear better clothes, why not eat better food?" (*LD*, 63). Similarly, Louise seeks in Marcus "another way to be free," knowing "she couldn't run away without [her father and brothers] bringing her back" (*LD*, 164). She is kept in a loveless marriage to Bonbon, made to stay there even as his involvement with Pauline grows deeper and more obvious to the plantation community.

Surprisingly, Louise harbors only a slight resentment for Pauline, and in its stead reveals a large amount of envy. She is jealous of Pauline not for having her husband but for having a vitality, strength, and confidence she lacks. Each description of Louise stresses her frailty, and her jealousy of Pauline's strength is symbolically expressed through the envy in her comparison of Pauline's sons with her own daughter Tite: "There was no mistaking about the children, they were . . . her daughter's brothers, but nothing like her daughter. They had all the life, Tite had none" (*LD,* 164). A premature infant, Tite is born with a weak heart and is destined to a fragile existence. In her daughter's inability to enjoy a healthy childhood, Louise sees her own weakness and inability to control her own life, and she blames Bonbon for both.

The resentment Louise does feel toward Pauline comes not from the expected source—a rivalry between two women for the affection of the same man—but from her perception of the ineffectual nature of their positions as women within their society: "She liked Pauline. . . . But she hated Pauline, too. Not because she wanted Pauline to give her back her husband. . . . She wanted to be free of her husband. But she knew she never would be free of him. If Pauline was white, then everything would be different. Bonbon would marry Pauline and she would be able to leave. But Pauline was not white, and there couldn't be any marriage" (164). Because she sees little hope for liberation, Louise resigns herself to waiting for an opportunity to escape the confinement of a life with a man who does not love her. Jim tells us she has a history of watching the black men of the plantation, no doubt wondering whether any would be reckless enough to disregard societal rules and assist in her scheme of retribution. Sensing that somehow he might fulfill her needs, she watches Marcus carefully, in a manner that prompts Jim to say, "I had seen her look at other black men in the quarter, but I had never seen her watch any like she was watching Marcus now" (*LD,* 56). Louise and Marcus enter into a mutually beneficial relationship as each seeks to enact a personal rebellion, but their presuming to shatter conventions by becoming lovers amounts to an act of hubris and seals their fate. As Louise's housekeeper, Aunt Margaret, forebodes, " 'Y'all go'n die right here. 'Specially him there. . . . There ain't nothing but death—a tree for him" (*LD,* 207).

Marcus's demise is expected from the beginning of the novel because history has taught us that in the time and place Gaines sets this work, for a black man to have a proud and rebellious nature made death a strong possibility, and for a black man to become involved with a white woman made death a certainty. From the start of the novel it is clear that Marcus will live by no principles but his own. The rare mention of his last name indicates that he is a loner with no familial or cultural ties and no regard for family, elders, or community. Though Jim addresses the old woman who reared Marcus as "Miss Julie," denoting his respect for age, Marcus ignores her and is even disrespectful to her. In the scene where she bids him good-bye as he goes to the Hebert plantation, Marcus reveals a contempt and insolence that will characterize him throughout the novel: "She went to Marcus and put her arms around him and started crying when he got ready to leave. She told him to be sure to come back and see her. . . . Marcus didn't say a word. He let her hold him and cry over him, but he didn't open his mouth. She followed us to the door and waved again. . . . Marcus didn't even look back" (*LD,* 18). In the unspoken disdain Marcus displays toward Miss Julie, there is a recapitulation of the quality that permeated the relationship between Jackson and his aunt, Charlotte, in *Catherine Carmier.* Both young men feel a confused mixture of affection for and hostility toward the women who reared them, and both in a sense transfer blame onto these women for the displacement they experience now. The meager advantages Charlotte and Julie were so hard-pressed to pass on to Jackson and Marcus have no meaning in a society that values neither young man, and both are frustrated by the chasm between past values and present situation.

Although not afforded the formal education Jackson has received, Marcus has acquired the education of an exploitative environment. His disrespect for humanity is a learned one, taught to him as a boy when his father deserts him, as an adolescent when a co-worker extorts money from him, and as a young man in jail when he witnesses other inmates being forced into oral sex. His exposure to the darker side of human nature and his concluding that "Jesus healed the sick and raised the dead, but He didn't stop people from taking your money" (*LD,* 251) have transformed him from a "model" Christian to a cynic with a flagrant disregard for the conventions of what he sees as a hypocritical and hostile society. His early life recalls the naturalistic works of Theodore Dreiser and Frank Norris, particularly their characters who are victims of both sociological pressures and their own carnal drives.

As Marcus's character develops, he becomes less a pawn of compulsions and more an individual mind struggling against inequity. He dedicates his life to disregarding mores designed to govern his actions and labels designed to signify him as subservient. Though a black field-worker, he rejects the symbols he feels mark him as a creature of servitude and shows his contempt for the plantation order by replacing the khaki pants usually worn by field-workers with a pink shirt and brown pants, the straw hat with a cap, and the brogans with black-and-white "low-cut" shoes. Dressed to project an air of defiance, he scorns Bonbon's attempts to "break" him. Jim frequently describes Bonbon mounted on his horse following Marcus so closely that Marcus feels the animal's breath on his neck, and each description preludes an increased resolve on Marcus's part to rebel and exact revenge through involvement with Bonbon's mistress, Pauline. His dress and his arrogant behavior signal to Bonbon and others that he will not adapt to the plantation system at the expense of what he perceives to be his self-esteem and manhood.

Marcus views the plantation hierarchy of the 1940s as sharing the racial ethic of the slavery system that gave rise to it, and he is determined to emancipate himself and savor the freedom that comes from shaping his own destiny.[6] The act that he feels will facilitate his liberation is a reflex response, however, and not an act initiated wholly from his own volition. At first, Marcus is driven to become involved with Louise Bonbon not out of actual desire or love for her, and not as yet out of a desire to protest his environment. Both these motivations evolve from the emasculation he experiences in his pursuit of Pauline.

Throughout the novel Marcus prides himself on his sexual prowess. Jim recalls his boast, "[O]nce he got after a woman she couldn't do a thing but fall for him" (*LD*, 56–57), and the woman he "gets after" is Pauline. He is smug in his anticipated conquest; after all, "how could a white man—no, not even a solid white man, but a bayou, catfish-eating Cajun—compete with him when it came down to loving" (*LD*, 57)? Implicit in Marcus's assessment of Bonbon as a "catfish-eating Cajun" is a disapprobation based on caste and power. To him, Bonbon is not a "real" white man but merely a pretender to the throne of white power, because he has not descended from the old lines of social power that a Marshall Hebert has. While Marcus has been made accustomed to the rule of established southern families, he sees in Bonbon a parvenu usurper and resents the authority given to Sidney and refused him. For Marcus, wielding sexual power ameliorates the denial of social and economic power. While Bonbon may exercise control over him in the fields, he believes his sexuality compensates for social impotence and makes him Bonbon's equal.

As Marcus levels Bonbon's status with his own, it becomes increasingly difficult for him to comprehend the attraction between Bonbon and Pauline. A disbelieving Marcus is left puzzling over how Pauline could prefer a white man to himself. He is outraged at her dismissal, for it encompasses a complete denial of his manhood, both sexually and socially. His turning to Louise for retribution allows him to retaliate against the white man he perceives has stripped him of the only power that society has allotted him, his illusion of irresistible maleness.

Louise has no presence for Marcus until Pauline spurns him. Jim tells us, "[Marcus] paid no more attention to her than he did a weed standing 'side the road" (*LD,* 75). As Bonbon comes to represent everything in his society that constrains him, Marcus's determination to rebel is strengthened, and Louise is transposed from a childlike woman to a siren luring him to revenge and certain death. In the course of their relationship Marcus grows to love Louise sincerely, but the rules of their racist society are a divine order with which their desires are in conflict. Their futile attempt to sustain an impossible union, the fear their relationship engenders throughout the community, and their subsequent ruin testify to the power of their social order.

Louise and Marcus's relationship is constantly viewed in terms of its impact on the quarters, and even the most intimate details of sexual frolic are rendered in the context of group condemnation. As the couple indulge in an elaborate foreplay with racial overtones, Aunt Margaret, Louise's black housekeeper, becomes a personification of communal disapprobation. Her actions symbolize both white social response to Marcus and Louise's relationship and black fear of the possible repercussions of their liaison. She listens to them through the closed door of Louise's bedroom, loudly articulating her disapproval while trying to break in the door to enter, and her efforts cast the couple's love in a surreal light, accentuating its social aberrance. Her shouts in answer to the noise from the banging of furniture in the bedroom create a bizarre ménage à trois in which all three characters are involved in a "call and response" lovemaking, Louise and Marcus as the actual participants and Aunt Margaret as the voice of societal censure. Aunt Margaret, Louise, and Marcus become elements of a tableau violently illustrating the ravishing of the status quo, and lovemaking is no longer an intimate association but an interaction of forces that threaten to reel out of control.

The sexual act between Marcus and Louise occurs in part 2 and significantly is preceded by an elaborately detailed brawl. At one of the "house fairs"—a fete held in the quarters—while the workers of the plantation are eating, drinking, and gambling, a riot rumbles, gains momentum, and erupts. There are no obvious reasons for the violence, and the fight appears to be a random release of human energy and anger that ends in chaos. The scene itself has no specific plot function but serves an important thematic function: symbolically, it is a prelude to the chaos that will result from the random forces of interracial love within this society. Marcus and Louise represent anarchy, but by novel's end the entropy caused by the couple's relationship is checked by the social order, and the inertia of racism remains.

The lovers pay dearly for violating a social taboo, but their fate comes as no surprise to the blacks of the plantation. From the onset of their illicit relationship a feeling of foreboding permeates the quarters as each character senses impending tragedy. Aunt Margaret, who attempts to protect Louise's daughter, Tite, from her mother's relationship with Marcus; the butler, Bishop, who attempts to protect the plantation owner, Marshall Hebert, from involving Marcus in a plan to eliminate Bonbon; and Jim, who attempts to protect Marcus from the consequences of his actions—all sense the danger ensuing from the existing state of affairs on the plantation. Further, all know the retribution that will follow.

Because of his relationship with Louise, Marcus inspires fear in every black person in the quarters. The community shifts its reaction to him, from disbelief that he would even consider a relationship with Louise, to fear when they realize he is a rebel out of control. While this is a community that can tolerate most types of human behavior, from single women who provide sexual services to the men of the community to a pair of homosexual lovers, it cannot tolerate any attempt to change the rules governing the predictability of its socioracial machinery. Fearing the uncertainty and violence of change, all members of the community conspire to stop Marcus: the gays attempt to outwork him in the field; Aunt Ca'line and Pa Bully, the older couple who are Pauline's neighbors, attempt to stop him from seeing Pauline; and Bishop slams the door in his face when he appears on Marshall Hebert's steps. As Bishop explains, "[A]ny black person who would stick his foot in a door that slavery built would do almost anything" (*LD*, 216). The blacks on the plantation observe a covenant with their oppressive society and know that the action of one could bring wrath on all, because all black men and women of the quarters are culpable for the actions of one. At the novel's end, the doom prophesied by Aunt Margaret and other blacks materializes.

Because Bonbon has committed murder for Hebert, he now holds the power of coercion over him. Hebert seeks to put an end to Bonbon's extortion and enlists Marcus in his scheme. In return, he promises Marcus money and protected flight with Louise. Realizing that in employing Marcus to this end he potentially risks substituting one blackmailer for another, Hebert simultaneously tells Bonbon of Marcus's affair with Louise, knowing that Sidney, though indifferent to Louise, must seek retribution to protect both his status as a white man and the sanctity of white femininity. He alerts Bonbon to the time Marcus plans to flee with Louise and Tite, and a

fight between Bonbon and Marcus ensues. As the novel moves toward its
conclusion, it is evident that the only one to actually benefit from the turn
of events is Marshall Hebert. Extending the analogy that likens this text to
the Greek tragedies, Hebert resembles the gods, "[t]he blessed immortals"
intimately involved with human affairs, who "may . . . if they feel so inclined, graciously stoop towards a mortal and assist him . . . [b]ut at any
moment . . . may turn away and reveal the immeasurable gulf which separates their state of blessedness from the anguish of those doomed to die"
(Lesky, 2). As a white landowner, Hebert symbolizes the omnipotence that
controls across lines of race and class. Everyone, from Marcus to Bonbon, is
manipulated by him, and Marcus's feeble attempt at resistance is no match
for the social power Hebert's ancestry gives him. The personal protest
Marcus mounts against the system Hebert upholds is rendered ineffectual,
for nothing on the plantation has changed: conditions within the quarters
are the same, and life within a system based on race and caste continues as if
Marcus's anger had never touched it. The only legacy left by his gesture of
rebellion is that which becomes apparent in the gradual transformation of
Jim's character.

At the beginning of the novel, Jim's unwillingness to "rock the boat" is a
refrain repeated as often as the blues lyrics he sings about his lost love, Billie
Jean. His emasculation by the rules he is unwilling to question initially
places him at odds with Marcus, who calls him a "whitemouth" and sees
Jim as a symbol of everything he refuses to be: an "Uncle Tom" who sub-
verts his dignity and self-esteem while resigning himself to a demeaning position, a man who puts his suffering into playing the blues "real slow and
sad" (*LD*, 50) rather than into action. As they discuss Hebert's proposal to
Marcus, we see how divergent their attitudes are toward the social order of
which they both are a part. Whereas Jim's vision of the plantation system
casts it as the least of the evils present in a society inherently weighted
against black men, Marcus's likens it to slavery:

"Do your work and forget all these deals. . . . All you can do is make things harder
for yourself and for everybody else around here."

"Things can't get harder for me, Jim. I'm a slave here now. And things can't get
harder than slavery."

"The pen can be harder."

"I ain't going to no pen. . . ."

"And that's why you ought to do as well as you can."

"Be a contented old slave, huh? . . ."

"You're not a slave here, Marcus. You're just paying for something you did."
(224–25)

Marcus does not view his tenure at the Hebert plantation as a punishment
for his taking the life of a black man, because he knows the small value his
society places on black life. Like Munford Bazille in "Three Men," he discerns the manipulative nature of the plantation system, and senses that
Hebert has freed him only for his own purposes. In the treatment he receives
at the hands of Bonbon and Hebert, Marcus sees a reincarnation of the system of slavery. Though its physical abuse and sale of human beings are absent, an identical psychological dehumanization is present.

Jim, on the other hand, accepts the institution of the plantation and his
place in it. He is accustomed to the world being a certain way and has inter-
nalized a racial hierarchy that says white *men* are in charge, not black men,
and in an interesting scene, certainly not black women. His acceptance of
white rule is evident throughout the novel, and his sexual conservatism is
evident in a telling instance when he realizes that Marcus's guardian, Miss
Julie Rand, has manipulated him into adopting a fatherly role toward
Marcus: "She was a little old gangster . . . and you expect this of white people. But she was my own race—and a woman, too" (*LD,* 14). Accustomed
to a certain order and regularity, he prefers not to have his perception of the
status quo upset.

Jim is passive and views the suffering he and others experience as the way
of the world. Even his conception of the relationship of man and God is
based on a tacit assumption that man is meant to struggle, while God, removed from the human plight, casually chooses to observe and act or not.
In his account of working the fields in sweltering heat, Jim's tone indicates
his reconcilement to life's drudgery as he hopelessly asks for a breeze as a
sign of good faith from the Lord: "Do You care? I don't think so—because
if You did, it looks to me like You would send us a little breeze. . . . Now,
mind you, I'm not asking You that for myself. . . . I figure a man with an
eight-grade education, with a sitting-down job, shouldn't go round com-
plaining about anything" (*LD,* 38). So resigned is he to his existence that
Jim deems himself fortunate to have an eighth-grade education and a
"sitting-down job." His acceptance contrasts sharply with Marcus's recalcitrance. Unlike Marcus, who actively demands more from his world, Jim is
appeased by its morsels and awaits God's action to bring about change. But
also unlike Marcus, Jim possesses compassion, as is implied in his statement
"I'm not asking you that for myself," and it is this concern for his community that makes him an ideally empathetic narrator.

Jim is not only a character; he is also a symbol of the philosophy and temperament of his community and their preferring to abide an inequitable situation rather than risk the uncertainty of change. Like the community whose life he chronicles, he finds it easier to take the path of least resistance, even when he is aware of blatant injustice. One example is his outrage at the practice of segregated drinking facilities, expressed only through resentment and procrastination:

I went around the other side and had myself a couple beers. You could buy soft drinks in the store, or if you were a white man you could drink a beer in there, but if you were colored you had to go to the little side room—"the nigger room." I kept telling myself, "One of these days I'm going to stop this. . . . I'm a man like any other. . . ." But I never did. Either I was too thirsty to do it, or after I had been working in the field all day I was just too tired and just didn't care. So I went around there and had a beer. (*LD*, 42–43)

Jim opts for the satisfaction of a cold beer on a hot day rather than the satisfaction of being able to drink that beer where he chooses. While it is certainly obvious that Jim's work is backbreaking, when taken in conjunction with the knowledge that he deems himself fortunate for having a "sitting-down job," his reasons for not objecting to his drinking status appear as excuses. Aware that the system is wrong, he prefers to rationalize his lack of reaction to injustice rather than take the more difficult route of enacting change.

Jim's complacency is shattered by Marcus's values and actions. As the two men observe each other's convictions and become friends, each influences the other, but Marcus has a much more profound influence on Jim. Through his demeanor and his deeds, he nudges Jim to the realization that besides resigned obeisance, there are alternative responses to the fear used by whites to maintain blacks in a state of impotence. As Marcus reveals his plan to kill Bonbon for Hebert, an extreme course of action by any standard, Jim naturally registers stupefaction as he strives to fathom the motivations that lead Marcus to such a radical deed. Yet even in his incredulity there is a nascent respect and admiration: "I leaned back . . . to look at Marcus. . . . I believed him because I remembered he had killed and it didn't mean a thing. I believed him because I remembered he had fooled that dog and jumped through that window to get to Bonbon's wife. I believed him because I remembered he had stuck his foot in that door—'that slavery had built'" (*LD*, 223). As he gazes at Marcus, Jim reviews each act of defiance Marcus has perpetrated: his initial murder that causes his tenure at the Hebert plantation, his intimacy with Louise, and his conspiracy with Hebert. The implications of these actions resound in Jim's consciousness, and he is struck by the distance his inaction has placed between him and his own dignity. With this dawning of perception, he comes to view Marcus in a new light, not as a young man with random disregard for societal rules and structures but as a rebel with a legitimate cause, the maintenance of self-esteem.

For the majority of the novel, Marcus's arrogance, selfishness, and lack of compassion make him an unsympathetic character, but Jim's new appreciation of him softens the negative reaction he generates. As he reveals what prompts Marcus, Jim creates a context in which Marcus's actions are understandable, if not excusable. Jim's changing perception is meant to encourage the reader's to change as well. When he refers to Marcus as "the bravest man I ever knew, the bravest man I had ever met" (*LD*, 270), Marcus is imbued with a different significance. He becomes more than an angry young man, and his union with Louise becomes more than a black man seeking revenge on his overseer: he is transposed into a tragic hero who becomes a man when questioning his fate. The tragic dimensions of Marcus's act are even more evident if we consider that "[t]he tragic hero stands out against a background of those who yield or avoid a decisive choice, his absolute determination is pitted against an overwhelming power; but in him the dignity of a great human being remains intact in defeat" (Lesky, 114). Marcus becomes a hero because he has fought for personal dignity. His desire for respect takes on larger dimensions once they effect a change, though only a modest one, in Jim. While working in the fields, knowing Marcus and Louise are leaving and he might not have the opportunity to say good-bye, Jim reflects, "I wanted to tell them that they were starting something . . . that others would hear about, and understand, and would follow. 'You are both very brave and I worship you,' I was going to say" (*LD*, 270).

Although their society contrives to destroy Marcus and Louise for their disobedience of its rules, their relationship gives Jim new insight into the structure of his society and courage to rethink his position in it. His growing social awareness is evident in his reflections as he enters the quarters looking for Marcus and Louise: "The whole place was so dark and quiet, it looked like everybody had moved away. But they hadn't moved away, they had locked themselves inside the houses. All of them had heard what Marcus was supposed to do and all of them were afraid. It was the same fear that made me hate Marcus at first. It was fear for myself and all the rest. The fear was still in me, but I didn't blame Marcus for it any more. Because it wasn't Marcus who was doing this; it was the big people" (*LD*, 270–71).

Jim's description of the fear that caused him and the entire community to resent Marcus gives a precise anatomy of the manner in which fear is used by those in control to check the responses of those they subjugate. His use of the phrase "big people" illustrates his perceptive appreciation of the small stature he is allowed in a society that demeans him.

Because of Marcus, Jim reevaluates his assessment of his world, and his new philosophy is imbued with Marxist overtones. He views Hebert's machinations as part of a grand design to maintain the separations intrinsic to race and class discrimination, and he now realizes that Hebert is the one he should fear and resent, not Marcus, or even Bonbon: "It's not Marcus, it's them. Marcus was just the tool. . . . Like Bonbon was the tool—put there to work Marcus. Like Pauline was a tool, like Louise was a tool" (LD, 269). With new insights, Jim is charged with the bravery to fashion his own quiet stance against the order that has caused the death of Marcus. When Marshall has rid himself of both Bonbon and Marcus, he suggests, under the guise of caring for Jim's welfare, that he leave the plantation. Although he says to Jim, "These Cajuns know you and that boy lived in the same house, and they might get it in their heads to do you something," it is evident to Jim that Marshall's concern is not for him but for Marshall himself: "He wasn't worried about the Cajuns hurting me. He wanted me to leave because I knew the truth about what had happened. He was afraid I might start blackmailing" (LD, 278). When Marshall attempts a payoff in the form of a letter of recommendation, Jim quietly reads it, refolds it, and returns it to Marshall, replying, "No Sir, I'll get by" (LD, 278). By rejecting Marshall's supposed offer of assistance, he rejects Marshall's manipulation and to a degree keeps what remains of his integrity intact.

Jim's gesture affords him a small amount of dignity and sadly constitutes the sum impact of Marcus's life. The closing scene in Of Love and Dust is a melancholy one that echoes the novel's title and reveals the near-negligible impression Marcus's attempted resistance has left on his community. His life, like dust, has no real substance and no real impact. In order for his act to matter, Marcus would have had to matter, and in a society in which he is deemed marginal and insignificant, he does not. In speaking of the novel's title, Gaines elaborates on the relationship of the symbol of dust to his theme: "Dust is the absence of love. Dust is the absence of life. Man goes back to dust when he dies. . . . These people wanted to love, but because of the way the system is set up, it was impossible to love" (Rowell, 43). The quotation from the minister's eulogy at Marcus's funeral—"Man is here for a little while, then gone" (LD, 281)—further accentuates the tragic vision of the insignificance of human life against a monolithic system. Not only is

Marcus's life of a fleeting nature, particularly since he decided to live it as a black man who would defer to none, but the imprint he has left is evanescent as well. Both black and white conspire to continue the debasement and degradation within the plantation system, the whites to ensure their power, the blacks to abide a constant evil rather than face the turmoil of change. As Aunt Margaret says in her closing conversation with Jim, "When you live as long as I done lived, you learn to forget things quite easy" (*LD,* 279), and most of the characters do forget Marcus and what he attempted. The underlying tragedy within this tragedy is that Marcus has inspired only one to take up the cause of human dignity.

However pessimistic the vision of the novel seems, the small impact Marcus makes on his society is appropriate to Gaines's vision of protest and change. For him, inspiring one is as important as inspiring many. His characters do not effect large social and racial transfigurations; they simply attempt to make sense of their personal world against the larger backdrop of society's forces. The most important battle they wage is that for their individual dignity; without this, no true social change will be possible or effective. Gaines's victors are quiet, solitary heroes and heroines who through small acts of personal pride set gradual change in motion. Marcus affects one man, but if we look at his action in terms of Gaines's larger canon, a momentum begins that will build and culminate in Gaines's next novel, as Jane Pittman affects many.

Ultimately, the tragedy of Marcus has its largest impact in its effect on the reader. We are stirred by the defenselessness of human beings against a racist social hierarchy; we are moved by individuals who at all costs strive to maintain dignity; and we are inspired to believe that even in a rural parish, change will come, perhaps not swiftly but quietly and eventually.

Chapter Five
From History to Her-story: *The Autobiography of Miss Jane Pittman*

> Truth to me is what people like Miss Jane remember.
> —Ernest Gaines

I had been trying to get Miss Jane Pittman to tell me the story of her life for several years now, but each time I asked her she told me there was no story to tell. I told her she was over a hundred years old, she had been a slave in this country, so there had to be a story. . . .

"What you want know about Miss Jane for?" Mary asked.

"I teach history," I said. "I'm sure her life's story can help me explain things to my students."

"What's wrong with them books you already got?" Mary said.

"Miss Jane is not in them."[1]

History is interpretation, and in this excerpt from the introduction to his most acclaimed work, *The Autobiography of Miss Jane Pittman,* the significance of historical vision for Ernest Gaines is tacitly but clearly articulated. Implied in this history teacher's desire to include Jane in his teaching is a need to expand history to include elements heretofore excluded or misrepresented. Standard histories have not always done justice to the rich cultural repositories of lives such as Jane's, and the fictional Miss Jane Pittman becomes a vehicle for Gaines's reinterpretation of her people's place in larger American history. The work transforms the African-American saga from—to borrow the terms used by Malcolm X—the "his-story" warped or neglected in traditional annals to the "my-story" of a folk epic.

Gaines is well aware of the interpretive nature of history as he constructs *Miss Jane.* While speaking of the research necessary to create the work, he reveals the divergence in perspectives on historical fact that race, class, and other sociocultural considerations can cause: "While talking to people and reading books, . . . I got different interpretations. The same results while reading the papers of the North and the papers of the South, or reading history books by black historians and by white historians" ("MJ and I," 36). Gaines weaves the various outlooks discovered in his research into a narrative that interprets history from a largely overlooked viewpoint, that of a black female.

It is noteworthy that Gaines invents a female narrator. Rarely has American history been chronicled through the perspective of a black woman, and to allow a black woman's voice to recall history is a striking act of fictional revision. The choice of a woman is fitting too, if we consider Gaines's characterization of the women in his works. Whether it is Octavia, who teaches her son how to survive in a segregated environment; the hoodoo woman, who teaches Eddie the true meaning of manhood; or Aunt Fe, who personifies the pride of her community—Gaines's women provide the nurture that enables individual, familial, and communal survival. Jane's character follows in this tradition and bears a strong resemblance to Aunt Fe. When first written, *Miss Jane* was entitled "A Short Biography of Miss Jane Pittman," and of her original conception Gaines states, "I had a group of people from a multiple point of view telling the story. And then I said, . . . this is too much like 'Just Like a Tree.' I've got the same characters telling the same thing. All I've done with Aunt Fe is that instead of her dying, I tell everything that happened before she died" (Ingram and Steinberg, 343). Where Jane most significantly differs from Fe is in the epic nature of her story. As much icon as character, she is the culmination of the unifying power Gaines gives to his female creations. Through her, others are able to connect their experiences to the recent and distant past, and her life is a composite of many episodes in larger black life. That her narrative recapitulates the stories of many is evident in the acknowledgment of Gaines's history teacher that precedes the text: "I should mention here that even though I have used only Miss Jane's voice throughout the narrative, there were times when others carried the story for her. . . . This is not only Miss Jane's autobiography, it is theirs as well. . . . Miss Jane's story is all of their stories, and their stories are Miss Jane's" (*MJP*, x). In Jane's authentic voice, many other heretofore-neglected histories are heard.

Jane's life spans the most significant periods of African-American history, and even though she is an invention her autobiography is intended as a symbolic reality. The history teacher who opens the work signs the end of his introduction "the editor," and the verisimilitude created here permeates the entire work. In crafting an editorial persona Gaines imagines an amanuensis who is simply recording the real story of Jane Pittman. His description

of subsequent reactions to the work indicates his level of success in rendering
Jane as a lifelike creation:

> Since the publication of *The Autobiography of Miss Jane Pittman* . . . I've read sev-
> eral reviews in which critics have called Miss Jane a real person. A representative of
> *Newsweek* asked me to send the editors of the magazine a picture of Miss Jane
> Pittman. . . . The actress Ruby Dee . . . also mistook Miss Jane for a real per-
> son. . . . One lady accused me of using a tape recorder, then calling the interview a
> novel after I had cut out all the inconsequential material. . . .
>   But *The Autobiography of Miss Jane Pittman* is absolute fiction. By that I mean I
> created Miss Jane, and if I did not create all the events she mentions in her narra-
> tive, I definitely created all the situations that she is personally involved in. ("MJ
> and I," 23)

The closing statement in this passage illustrates an interesting duality in
Gaines's conception of himself as a writer. Even though he is concerned with
re-creating reality and humbly acknowledges, "Once the story really got
moving, Miss Jane did and said pretty much whatever she wanted, and all I
could do was act as her editor" ("MJ and I," 37), he makes it clear that it is
the writer, conscious of technique, who has created Jane and the manner in
which she reacts to the situations that touch her. In her story he achieves a
delicate balance between his respect for the reality from which Jane's story
derives and his respect for the art of fiction to which he as a writer is bound.
The result is a blending of storyteller and writer, as the written form is over-
laid with the strong, personal voice of Miss Jane.

The rhetorical strategies of orality are vital to the construction of Jane's
narrative, and her story is firmly rooted in the oral tradition. When the history teacher states, "What I have tried to do here was not to write everything, but in essence everything that was said," the emphasis on recording
Jane's recall of moments *and* her act of speaking is made clear. Memory itself can be too evanescent, for when thoughts exist only in the mind they are
subject to loss. Only through speaking, through giving thoughts verbal
form, can a consistent and concrete reality be constructed and passed on.
Jane conveys the events of her life as gathered knowledge (appropriately, to
a history teacher who will ensure its perpetuity by passing it on to a new
generation of blacks represented in his students), and her story effects cultural continuity.

To ensure that he has crafted a realistic voice for Jane, Gaines acknowledges that he has taken for a model *Lay My Burden Down,* the collection of
Work Projects Administration interviews of ex-slaves: "I used that book to

get the rhythm of speech and an idea of how the ex-slaves would talk about themselves" (Rowell, 46–47). A comparison of a passage taken from *Lay My Burden Down* and a similar one from *The Autobiography* shows how much the narrative of former slaves shaped Jane's language:

> When my race first got they freedom and begin to leave they marses, a heap of the marses got raging mad and just tore up truck. They say they gwine kill every nigger they find. Some of them did do that very thing, boss, sure enough. I's telling you the truth. They shot niggers down by the hundreds. They just wasn't gwine let 'em enjoy their freedom. That is the truth, boss.[2]

Jane's description of the same event reads as follows:

> The old masters didn't think too much of it at first. They was glad the niggers was leaving. If they got rid of all the bad niggers—them the only ones leaving anyhow—if all of them left there wouldn't be no more trouble. They didn't know it at first, but it wasn't just the bad ones leaving. . . . Now, the old masters came back and tried to force the people to stay. They turned the Klans loose on them, the Camellias, and the White Brotherhood loose on the people. (*MJP*, 72)

The cadences of former slaves are undeniably present in Jane's narrative, and her expression is faithful to that of her realistic counterparts. Their simple sentences, their repetition to underscore points and provide continuity—such elements are all reproduced in her speech, as is evident in her description of a colonel dwarfed by his role of leadership in the Confederate army: "The Secesh Army, they came by first. . . . The Officers on their horses, the Troops walking. . . . The colonel was a little man with a gun and a sable. The sable was so long it almost dragged on the ground. Looked like the colonel was a little boy who had got somebody else's sable to play with" (3–4). The humor in Jane's depiction of the colonel overwhelmed by his position does not occur frequently in other historical sources or in the polemical works that analyze slavery and the Civil War. It is unique to this autobiographical narrative in which an insider's intimate perceptions and observations add another dimension to history. It bears noting that Gaines stated he used *Lay My Burden Down* not only to assist in achieving linguistic verisimilitude but also to give insight into how ex-slaves would talk *about themselves*. As much as recalling the language of former slaves, *Jane Pittman* also reveals what might have been their vision of the world.

When Charles Nichols states in his introduction to *Many Thousand Gone*, "Nearly everyone concerned with American slavery has had his say, but in our time we have forgotten the testimony of its victims," he describes the intent of his work as giving a history of slavery told "essentially from the point of view of those whose unpaid labor maintained the plantation system."[3] The following questions he uses in creating his documentary assist in understanding the design of *Jane Pittman*:

What does it mean to be another man's property? How does it feel to work without wages, or, as a field hand, coerced into producing another's cotton, corn, or sugar, to be forced in all society's arrangements to accept the blight of inferiority? What imaginings stirred the minds of these illiterate and brutalized men? What emotions inflamed their murderous and abortive revolts? When compelled into submission and disingenuous cooperation, what was the nature of their tenuous "adjustment" to slavery? Or having fled the plantation, what had slavery done to their personality and behavior? These are questions which only the slave . . . can directly answer. . . . Although a few histories of slavery have employed some . . . autobiographies as sources, there is no . . . work presenting the plantation system from the slaves' point of view. Above all, there is no intimate study of the psychology of the enslaved. (Nichols, ix)

In a fictionalized form, *Jane Pittman* becomes the intimate portrait Nichols describes.

Jane's autobiography gives a detailed, interior view of a familiar epoch, and the uniqueness and veracity of her voice compel the reader into an imaginary union with her historic vision. Her choice of words, selection of details, and inclusion of many asides allow her to capture general, regional, and personal histories. Her recalling the series of teachers employed to instruct the black children of her plantation is an example. As she reviews the nature of education on her plantation, Jane digresses momentarily to tell the story of the Creole family, the LeFabres. By placing a family's experience, views, and values in the middle of a general history of black education on a postbellum plantation, she gracefully includes a supplementary component, the color division within Creole society, that gives her story a distinct Louisiana flavor. Jane also employs temporal markers specific to her Louisiana world to lend order to the diverse events of her history. In recalling larger events, such as the institution of sharecropping and the fight for civil rights, she uses signposts, such as the election and death of Huey P. Long and the floods of 1917 and 1927, as narrative guides. Both her asides and her markers are traditional devices used to structure oral narrative, but they are crafted to give history a regional and personal perspective.[4] Jane's memory unfolds an alternative to the standard and reminds us that history is made up of diverse individuals. Slavery, Reconstruction, and the beginnings of the civil rights movement are all documented through the language, art forms, mythology, spirituals, and folk sermons of one woman and her immediate community.

Book 1 of the narrative of this singular woman begins with the era that has most influenced African-American experience in the United States, slavery. Entitled "The War Years," this section of the work is given over to Jane's concrete descriptions of her life as a bondwoman. The horrendous details of barbarity and dehumanization present in other accounts of the slave system are present here, but Jane's treatment of these details is somewhat different. She reveals not only the facts of slavery but also her personal thoughts and reactions to the experience of bondage. Her account is given greater power by comments and analyses depicting both slavery's inhumanity and the manner in which slaves sought to overcome dehumanization. Every facet of "the peculiar institution" is individualized within Jane's narrative, and historic wrongs against a mass of people that might have remained abstract in other historical documents become keenly felt, immediate wrongs against a character so real she seems alive. Her vivid portraits render the horrors of slavery even more abhorrent because they occur to a character whose psyche we know so intimately.

Jane's descriptions reveal an acute, active mind that immediately counters the stereotype of the ignorant, unfeeling slave. In recounting her experience while bringing water to Confederate soldiers, she articulates a slave's perception of the lack of significance chattel status imposes: "They couldn't tell if I was white or black, a boy or a girl. They didn't even care what I was" (*MJP,* 4). Jane's matter-of-fact tone as she details the casual denial of her presence constitutes a vivid reminder that the disavowal of a slave's humanity was routine. A subsequent description of a similar encounter contrasts sharply to this earlier episode in which Jane is objectified. In this account Jane brings water to a thirsty Union legion, and soldiers unsympathetic to her status as a human being are replaced by those who acknowledge her existence. One even confers a symbolic token of that acknowledgment, a name. Through Jane's joy, we see what the act of choosing a name comes to symbolize: the possibility of defining identity. She is so taken with the name and the gallantry of the Union soldier who gives it to her that both become representations of the distant ideal of freedom she subsequently seeks upon emancipation.

The action of the Union soldier tempers the denial of personal identity through the denial of such vital personal rights as the prerogative to choose one's name. Though yet another white man arbitrarily changes her name from Ticey to Jane Brown because, as the soldier says, "Ticey is a slave name" (*MJP*, 8), this process is different for Jane. The soldier's altering a label of slavery reveals a new world of control to her, one in which the power of the master, in this case manifested through naming, is not final. A name is chosen for her, but for the first time in her life Jane has the option of deciding whether or not she will retain it. Her jubilation in having a choice and a name she perceives as not being rooted in slavery is expressed when she says, "I just stood there grinning. . . . It was the prettiest name I had ever heard" (*MJP*, 9).

Jane pays a high price for her new appellation, and in her subsequent recalcitrance we see the power of nomenclature to confer personal identity and pride, the very characteristics the system of slavery sought to suppress. As her master and mistress punish her for insubordination, the self-esteem she derives from choosing her own name mitigates the arbitrary brutality used to enforce their power within the slave system:

I raised my head high and looked her straight in the face and said: "You called me Ticey. My name ain't no Ticey no more, it's Miss Jane Brown. . . ." That night . . . she told my master I had sassed her. . . . My master told two of the other slaves to hold me down. . . . My master jecked up my dress and gived my mistress the whip and told her to teach me a lesson. Every time she hit me she asked me what I said my name was. I said Jane Brown. She hit me again: what I said my name was. I said Jane Brown.

My mistress got tired of beating me and told my master to beat me some. He told her that was enough, I was already bleeding. (*MJP*, 9)

By demanding to be called not only by a new name but also by the title "Miss," Jane demands respect and recognition of an existence apart from that of a slave.

For Jane, sovereignty in naming lessens the degradation of her life and sustains the dream of someday controlling her own destiny. She discards the label that was a symbol of her enslavement and adopts one that will serve as the icon of her freedom. Jane is not the only slave for whom naming represents the sovereignty of one's destiny. After emancipation, each of the newly freed slaves of her plantation disposes of the name given by the master and selects his or her own. She recalls the moment in the following manner: "We must have been two dozens of us there, and now everybody started changing names. . . . Nobody was keeping the same name Old Master had gived them" (*MJP*, 17–18). The slaves' first step toward freedom is the seizing of their personal identities. Like Jane, they too view the reappropriation of their personal details to be the prelude to reappropriation of personal destiny.[5]

As Jane's narrative continues, she relates one of the most important aspects of black life after slavery, the journey to freedom. In earlier preemancipation African-American literature, fear of jeopardizing the safety of those seeking liberation and those assisting in its attainment made precise descriptions of journeys to freedom a rarity. Though her account unfolds after emancipation, Jane's recall furnishes a possible likeness of this often-absent chapter in slave literature. While she is no longer a slave, her freedom is tenuous at best, and her descriptions of heading north contain perils similar to those alluded to in many slave narratives. She recalls in detail the former slaves' fear, their hope, and the rather cryptic freedom that existed for them after the Civil War: "We didn't know a thing. We didn't know where we was going, we didn't know what we was go'n eat. . . . We didn't know where we was go'n sleep that night. If we reached the North, we didn't know if we was go'n stay together or separate. We had never thought about nothing like that, because we had never thought we was go'n ever be free. Yes, we had heard about freedom, we had even talked about freedom, but we never thought we was go'n ever see that day" (*MJP*, 16). Not having any hope for freedom, Jane did not need a clear conception of liberty. The systematic debasement of slavery was designed in part to make certain that no slave was prepared for the advent of freedom; therefore, considerations of future action were few because emancipation was a remote ideal rather than a reality. Though very much a realist, Jane falls prey to simplifying freedom, thinking that emancipation included the provision of such basic necessities as food, shelter, and clothing. Ironically, her position comes very close to exemplifying the argument used by "benevolent" slaveholders for the continuance of "the peculiar institution": that slaves were docile, witless innocents incapable of self-preservation. Jane's thoughts and life belie that argument, however, and debunk the popular myth of black helplessness.

The shock of freedom's reality first jars Jane when she discovers that emancipation not only entails heretofore-denied responsibility but also bestows a nebulous freedom that guarantees no human rights. The intoxication of liberation is replaced by the sobriety of a slave's tenuous existence when she hides in a thicket, watching as fellow slaves are massacred by former members of the slave patrols and former Confederate soldiers. In this powerful and moving scene, Jane describes the remnants of the band of slaves in her usual matter-of-fact tone and underscores the similarity between antebellum and postbellum brutality: "I saw people laying everywhere. All of them was dead or dying, or so broken up they wouldn't ever move on their own" (*MJP*, 23). The scene gathers power as Jane recalls her reaction and the reaction of the little boy she informally adopts, Ned, to the killing of his mother and little sister.

At this point in her narrative, Jane is a child of 11 and Ned is even younger. One is struck by their stoicism as much as by the violence and brutality of the murder. Both remain collected during the massacre, and Jane has the presence of mind to hide Ned, while he has the presence of mind to remain quiet. As she says of him, "Small as he was he knowed death was only a few feet away" (*MJP*, 22). Slavery has forced a mature awareness of death upon the children. Loss of life and fragmentation of family are everyday occurrences, and Jane and Ned are prepared to deal with both as unfortunate eventualities.

Jane continues to recall the aftermath of this episode, and the lack of self-pity in her tone, as well as her determination to survive, typifies her character throughout the autobiography. Her discovery of the remains of Ned's mother, Laura, and his sister is rendered in a manner that illustrates the fortitude of her psyche:

Then I saw Big Laura. She was laying on the ground with her baby still clutched in her arms. . . . Even before I knelt down I saw that her and the baby was both dead.

I took the baby out her arms. I had to pull hard to get her free. I knowed I couldn't bury Big Laura . . . but maybe I could bury her child. But when I looked back at Big Laura and saw how empty her arms was, I just laid the little baby right back down. I didn't cry, I couldn't cry. I had seen so much beating and suffering; I had heard about so much cruelty in those 'leven or twelve years of my life I hardly knowed how to cry. (*MJP*, 23)

Slavery's harshness endows Jane with a resolve that might seem to border on indifference but in actuality constitutes a protective psychological mechanism. At the early age of 11 she knows that "[w]e couldn't let what happened yesterday stop us today" (*MJP*, 25), and she will not allow herself to bemoan the atrocities of her past, but rather forces herself to attempt to forge a future of freedom. After the massacre she gathers herself and Ned to continue their journey North and reasons pragmatically, "I thought we might as well take some of the grub that was left there" (*MJP*, 23).

Viewing the killing of Laura, her baby, and the other ex-slaves matures Jane and alters her conception of freedom, but only somewhat. She is still unaware of the vast geographical distance that stands between her and Ned and the freedom they seek in the North. Her naïveté is evident in her misguided sense of direction, which tells her Ohio is a week's walk from Louisiana. She sets off, actually walking farther south, and a series of picaresque episodes follow, commenting on segments of southern society during Reconstruction. Each is a symbol, and each teaches Jane of the difficulties of freedom: the black hunter seeking his father symbolizes fragmented families and tells Jane freedom "ain't North" (54);[6] an eccentric old white man reveals the hypocrisy of Jane's freedom and tells her that at her present rate it will take her "about thirty years. Give or take a couple" (54) to reach freedom; and a poor white farmer who by refusing to fight "their war" (56) symbolizes the class conflict among whites during the Civil War leads Jane and Ned to tenuous shelter on a plantation run by the newly formed Freedman's Bureau. Jane's path from one encounter to the next becomes a circular route returning her to where she began, the plantations of Louisiana, and her circuitous movement back to her origins dramatizes Gaines's concept of freedom and progress. She returns "home" because, in his view, true liberation and the progress it engenders are not an abstract, such as the notion of "freedom," or a spatial entity, such as "the North," but rather a spiritual entity, deeply rooted in a person's character, dignity, and knowledge of his or her history and place. With the exception of one segment, the remainder of Jane's story takes place in the parishes of Louisiana that provide the setting for other Gaines works and details the personal choices she makes to progress toward spiritual freedom.

Book 2 of Jane's memoir, entitled "Reconstruction," achieves exactly that, a reconstruction of significant historical events in a new context. In her rendering of the epoch after the Civil War, the upheaval of the southern social order and the new relationship of North to South shift from a central position and become backdrops for Jane's observations of the similarities between slavery and Reconstruction. In describing sharecropping, Jane reveals it as the reincarnation of slavery. The exploitation, absence of regular education, and denial of human rights that typified one now typify the other: "It was slavery again, all right. No such thing as colored troops, colored politicians, or a colored teacher anywhere near the place. . . . You had to give Colonel Dye's name if the secret group stopped you on the road. Just because the Yankee troops and the Freedom Beero had gone didn't mean they had stopped riding. They rode and killed more than ever now. . . . Yankee money came in to help the South back on her feet—yes; but no Yankee troops. We was left there to root hog or die" (*MJP,* 70). Jane's characterization of the North contrasts sharply to her early idealized vision of a place filled with citizens sympathetic to the plight of African Americans. She is now clearly aware of a North uninterested in racial equality and seeking only to rebuild a southern economy and reunite it with that of the

North. For black Americans still uneducated, still hunted by secret patrols, and still monitored strictly, the "North" as an entity had changed little. Through the institution of sharecropping, economic servitude replaced physical servitude, and the negation of humanity remained constant. In detailing her and her husband Joe's efforts to free themselves from the trap of tenant farming, Jane makes it evident that extricating oneself from economic bondage was almost as difficult as extricating oneself from physical bondage.[7] The intimacy characterizing Jane's view of the slavery epoch is continued in her descriptions of tenant farming.

In addition to revealing the historical inequity of sharecropping, Jane and Joe's story extends the universal content of *Miss Jane* by embodying concerns as diverse as the myth of the American West and *Moby-Dick*. Joe Pittman is described as "a real man" by Jane, and her own strength gives this phrase particular power. A cowboy and horse breaker, he seeks a more genuine freedom than that allowed in Louisiana. Emancipation has freed him from actual physical bondage, but he now seeks a liberation from the demeaning confines of sharecropping. After extricating himself from the perpetual debt of tenant farming, he does as other American heroes have done, goes west seeking greater opportunity. Jane's account of his experience continues her revision of American history by adding yet another forgotten chapter, the story of the black cowboy.

In *The Negro Cowboys* authors Philip Durham and Everett L. Jones describe the greater latitude offered to blacks in the West and give background for understanding why Joe desires to make Texas his home:

It would, of course, be ridiculous to say that there was no discrimination when men of different races worked together, particularly when most of them were Texans during the bitterness of Reconstruction and post-Reconstruction. But the demands of their job made them transcend much of their prejudice. On a drive, a cowboy's ability to do his work, to handle his share and a little extra, was far more important than his color. To be a good cowboy, one needed first of all to be a good man, for a wild longhorn had no more respect for a white Texan than for a Negro.

An old economic reality helped, too. When there are more jobs than men to fill them, there is less discrimination. And in the beginning, with literally millions of cattle and few experienced cowboys, trail bosses could not afford the luxury of unbridled discrimination. Many contemporary accounts show that some of the best riders, ropers, wranglers, and cooks were Negroes.[8]

Joe settles in the West, and the unfolding of his story counteracts the invisibility that became the fate of black cowboys "when history became myth and legend, when the cowboys became folk heroes, [and] the Negroes were again fenced out. They had ridden through the real West, but found no place in the West of fiction" (Durham and Jones, 2). In *Miss Jane* this valuable history now finds a place.

Breaking horses, Joe finds a life qualitatively different from that of the plantation. As he acts out his desire for greater freedom against the tableau of the western frontier, he comes to resemble another major figure in American letters who tackles the frontier of the sea, Ahab of Herman Melville's *Moby-Dick*. In the manner of Ahab, who rejects the slavery of the shore, Joe rejects the confinement of the plantation and pursues his destiny. Whereas Ahab's fight with his own destiny takes the form of his quest for the white whale, Joe's takes the form of breaking a black stallion. In pitting Joe against a wild horse that ultimately destroys him, Gaines admits to having Herman Melville in mind: "I was thinking of Moby Dick when I did the horse. I was thinking that nobody should break him, but then I thought, well, . . . Moby Dick gets away, and the horse should be broken somehow" (Ingram and Steinberg, 339).

Jane describes Joe's nemesis in mythical terms:

Tall, slick and black, . . . stronger and faster than any horse [Joe] had ever seen. Run for days and wouldn't get tired. Leap over a canal that a regular horse wouldn't even try. After they had been after him about a week some of the men started saying he was a ghost. Maybe even a haint. . . .

But they cornered him in the mountains. Joe said after they had caught him every last man there looked hurt. Hurt because the chase was over; hurt because they had to break him. (*MJP,* 90–91)

In battling the stallion Joe exemplifies the Ahab-like desire to control that which is beyond human control. He begins to define his manhood and subsequently his existence in terms of the horse and becomes obsessed with breaking the stallion. As she watches his increasing monomania, Jane intuits tragedy and consults the local hoodoo woman, who explains Joe's behavior as follows: "Man must always search somewhere to prove himself. He don't know everything is already inside" (*MJP,* 94). Because Joe seeks his selfhood in something outside himself, his fate is the same as Ahab's. But as Jane reflects on Joe's death, what she remembers is a Joe who had the courage to confront destiny at all costs. Gathering strength from his memory, she leaves Texas, returns to Louisiana, and subsequently confronts her own destiny.

The Jane who continues her narrative in Louisiana is a Jane more aware of society and the tenuous position she occupies within it. She has matured, and her autobiography increasingly includes acute analyses of the social significance attached to the events of her life. Her recounting the assassination of Ned, for example, is an instance of her revealing both her pain at the loss of her son and the factors that made his killing a certainty. His death follows Joe's and is the second of three key losses (the third being the killing of Jimmy Aaron) that bring Jane closer to confronting unfairness and becoming a symbol of leadership for her people.

Throughout her narrative, Jane reminds us that Ned remembers his mother, his sister, and the manner in which they died. His knowledge of his past and his awareness of current injustice instill in him a desire to effect change, a desire that subsequently makes him a threat to the sharecropping system. When Ned returns to his plantation, he is closely watched. His opening a school for black students and his lecturing the general black populace on the necessity for change make him a subversive influence that must be removed, and he is executed by the Cajun Albert Cluveau, an assassin hired by the local plantation owners. In narrating the events of the investigation that followed Ned's death, Jane lucidly depicts a legal system that provides no recourse for her and unjustly provides refuge for Cluveau: "The sheriff came and examined the body and asked Bam and Alcee some questions. They told him it was Albert Cluveau— . . . like he didn't already know it was Albert Cluveau, like everybody round there didn't already know it was Albert Cluveau. . . . He asked them if they wanted to call a Godfearing man like Mr. Albert Cluveau a liar. They said no. He told them to go on back home and he didn't want hear that kind of talk out of them no more" (*MJP*, 117–19). Reflecting upon the circumstances of Ned's death allows Jane to illuminate the social and racial order of her time. Her ruminations set the tone for the third book of the autobiography, which is more narrowly focused on her social observations.

In book 3, "The Plantation," Jane's narrative moves forward in time, fleshing out life on Samson plantation, her last home. She relates stories of the people of the quarters, and larger historic and current events recede from prominence and assume the place of backdrops. Taken as a whole, these recollections serve as modified allegory, illuminating particular aspects of black culture. In the section entitled "Miss Lilly," for example, Jane tells about the stern Lilly, "a bowlegged mulatto woman," whose aspirations for the children of the quarters force her to impose a value system inappropriate to their day-to-day reality of sharecropping: "She didn't just want lesson, she wanted the girls to come there with their dresses ironed, she wanted ribbons in their hair. The boys had to wear ties, had to shine their shoes. Brogans or no brogans, she wanted them shined" (*MJP*, 151). Teachers are a valuable commodity in Jane's world, and rare. Lilly, unfortunately, seems to be more concerned with the outward appearances of her charges than with their inward edification, and Jane uses her to illustrate the belief that education must be utilitarian and relevant to be successful. Lilly's story also signifies the obstacles faced in schooling rural black children who must eke out an education between the harvesting of crops.[9] Further, the number of teachers assigned to the plantation makes clear that the ignorance mandated by law in slavery is now perpetuated in a more benign manner: "After Miss Lilly, then came Hardy. Joe Hardy was one of the worst human beings I've ever met. . . . Telling poor people the government wasn't paying much, so he would 'preciate it if they could help him out some. . . . For a year and a half we didn't have a school on the place at all. Going into the second year we got that LeFabre girl" (*MJP*, 154–55). The "LeFabre girl" Jane refers to is Mary Agnes LeFabre, a Creole woman who comes to Jane's plantation to escape the strict doctrines of her Creole society. In recalling her history on the plantation, Jane creates a modified allegory that illuminates the complexities of the color line and the self-hatred that engendered it.

Relating the experiences of Mary Agnes, Jane's narrative echoes earlier Gaines themes, the social opposition to love across racial lines in *Of Love and Dust* and the rigid codes confining Creole women of color in *Catherine Carmier.* Mary Agnes's lineage both portrays the senseless color demarcations that use such phrases as "one drop" to define race and exemplifies the sexual exploitation of Creole women: "Mary Agnes LeFabre come from a long line of Creoles back there in New Orleans. Her grandmother was one drop from being white herself. Her grandmother had been one of these ladies for white men. They used to give these great balls before the war, and the white men used to go there to choose their colored women. They didn't marry these women, but sometime they kept them the rest of their life" (*MJP*, 155–56). Unable to abide by their values, Mary Agnes leaves her Creole community, but her arrival at Samson plantation sets in motion a chain of events that is the legacy of the history Jane describes above.

When she arrives at Samson to teach, Mary Agnes attracts the attention of Robert Samson, Jr., the young heir to the plantation, whose confused position within the hierarchy of race is symbolized through his having a black half-brother in the quarters whom he loves and plays with but whom he can never openly acknowledge as his brother. Robert's naïveté allows him to fall deeply in love with Mary Agnes and to disregard the dictates of his social position. Jane describes his feelings for her as sincere ones, saying, "[H]e didn't look at her the way you think a white man look at a nigger

woman. . . . He looked at her with love, and I mean the kind that's way
deep inside of you" (*MJP,* 169). As in *Of Love and Dust,* however, the social
order of the plantation system will not tolerate such love. Robert's feelings
for Mary Agnes only forebode ill and subsequently lead to tragedy. His
godfather, Jules Raynard, sums up his fate: "We know what everybody else
know in this parish, and that's he loved her. And because she couldn't love
him back, because she knowed better, he killed himself" (*MJP,* 186). Jane's
story of Robert and Mary Agnes allegorizes the inflexibility of a racial system that maintains its hierarchy even at human expense.

Personal recollections with overtones of social allegory are only part of
Jane's commentary. As she continues to divulge the details of her history,
she makes larger American history a living and present process. Important
figures of the American past are not two-dimensional portraits housed in
history books but human beings who impact on the lives of other human
beings such as Jane. The immediacy in her description of Frederick
Douglass is an instance: "Now, after the Yankee soldiers and Freedom Beero
left, the people started leaving again. Not right away—because Mr.
Frederick Douglass said give the South a chance. But when the people saw
they was treated just as bad now as before the war they said to heck with Mr.
Frederick Douglass and started leaving" (*MJP,* 71). In Jane's portrait
Frederick Douglass is not the great orator, abstracted and removed from his
cultural roots. Instead he is demythologized and shown to be part of a people's daily life as they attempt to make decisions that will form their history
and future.

Philosophical debates are also made intimate when Jane relates how
Ned, now adopting the surname of Douglass, has encouraged his students
to contemplate and argue the doctrines of W. E. B. Du Bois and Booker T.
Washington: "Professor Douglass. . . . You keep saying we ought to not listen to Mr. Washington, but ain't Mr. Washington saying that to keep the
race from getting slaughtered? Mr. Washington growed up round these
white people. He know a white man'll shoot a black man down just for
standing on two feet. . . . And another thing, Professor Douglass, . . . ain't
he saying learn a trade because a trade is the thing that's go'n carry this
country?" (*MJP,* 110). The theoretical debate over the importance of aca-
demic education versus vocational training, of which Booker T. Washington
was a key figure, is given human dimensions when people not only address
Washington's philosophy but refer to him as a man intimately steeped in
their culture.[10]

The immediate presence that Jane's revisionist narrative gives to black
American historical figures it also gives to white American figures. Her the-

ory explaining the death of Huey P. Long is an example: "What they think the rich people killed Long for? Because he called the colored people nigger? They killed him for helping the poor, the poor black and the poor white. Because you're not suppose to help the poor. Let the poor work, let the poor fight in your wars, then let them die. But you're not suppose to help the poor" (*MJP,* 149). Jane applies her own perspective to the popular account offered for Huey Long's death and constructs an analysis more in keeping with her history. She transcends questions of race and makes a strong argument with Marxist overtones, concluding that racism is no more than a diversion created by the rich and designed to encourage friction among the various ethnic elements of the poor, thus dissipating their energy to fight their real and common oppressor.

The personal interpretation Jane gives to history she also gives to traditional Christian religion, and her religion answers the hollow proclamations of the ministers in previous Gaines works. A spiritual woman, she is not awed by religious conventions. She will as soon sit before the radio to listen to Jackie Robinson play baseball on a Sunday as go to church. Her reverence for religion and its symbols is balanced by day-to-day realism, and she keenly feels that worship should not be divorced from life. The use of biblical images and terminology to mark the daily events of life on Samson plantation underscores Jane's pragmatic spiritualism, and the Bible's language is no longer remote but instead provides a fitting lexicon for describing significant periods in black history. The term *exodus,* for example, is used to refer to black migration: "Droves after droves . . . was leaving. If you went to town you would see whole families going by. Men in front with bundles on their backs, women following them with a child in their arm and holding another one by the hand. . . . They slipped away at night, they took to the swamps, they . . . went" (*MJP,* 72). Jane is a realist and sees that the stories of the Bible are meant as examples. She discerns its mythic nature, viewing its accounts as attempts to explain natural phenomena, the origin of humankind, traditions, and rituals. It is thus easy for her to see relevancy and importance in both the teachings of the Bible and the myths that derive from her own culture. Figures of African-American lore are given as much prominence as biblical figures in Jane's narrative. The former interact intimately with her community, and the immediacy of their presence is incorporated into her episodes. In Jane's encounter with the hoodoo woman Madame Eloise Gautier, we see that the legendary hoodoo queen Marie Leveau and her daughter are made integral parts of the communal psyche:[11] "The hoo-doo lived on a narrow little street called Dettie street. . . . She was a big mulatto woman, and she had come from New Orleans. At least that

was her story. She had left New Orleans because she was a rival of Marie
Laveau. Marie Laveau was the Queen then, you know, and nobody dare
rival Marie Laveau. Neither Marie Laveau mama, neither Marie Laveau
daughter who followed her. Some people said the two Maries was the same
one, but, of course, that was people talk" (*MJP,* 91–92). Consistently,
whether recalling historical events, analyzing biblical parables, or recounting
the doings of legendary figures, Jane's insights join the folk and the mythic
in a unique historic vision.

The sensibility that informs Jane's worldview extends Gaines's use of the
pastoral to this work. Like the characters of *Catherine Carmier,* Jane ardently feels a sympathy with her landscape. In the chapter "Of Men and
Rivers" her description of the relationship of people of color to the water-
ways that are part of their environment is an example: "The damage from
that high water was caused by man, because he wanted to control the rivers,
and you cannot control water. The old people, the Indians, used to worship
the rivers till the white people came here and conquered them and tried to
conquer the rivers too" (*MJP,* 145). Jane's references to contrasting cultural
visions of land politicize the treatment of nature within this work. More so
than in *Catherine Carmier* nature is linked to issues of social justice. When
she describes African-American and native American reverence for rivers
and fish, her account equates the social control exerted by whites with their
attempted control of nature by the building of artificial concrete levees:

So they tell me the Indians used to respect the rivers. . . . But when the white man
came here . . . he conquered the Indians. . . . After he had killed them he tried to
conquer the same river they had believed in, and that's when the trouble really
started.

I don't know when the first levee was built—probably in slavery time; but from
what I heard from the old people the water destroyed the levee soon as it was put
there. Now, if the white man had taken heed to what the river was trying to say to
him then, it would have saved a lot of pain later. But instead of him listening—no,
he built another levee. . . . Here the river been running for hundreds of years . . . till
the white man came here and tried to conquer it. (*MJP,* 146)

Just as the levee seeks to confine and rule the water, so do whites seek to
confine and rule African-American and native American peoples. This portion of the autobiography draws a continuous parallel between the abuse of
nature and that of people of color in the United States.

From Jackie Robinson to Marie Laveau to nature, all the elements of
Jane's narrative show her life to be a microcosm of the vast panorama of

African-American culture—its people, its history, its myth, its vision. She is a personified archive that in the first two books of her narrative records the African-American past and her place in it, and in the third provides an insightful commentary on African-American and larger American society. The fourth and last book of her autobiography, "The Quarters," is not so much a record of the past as a blueprint for the future. Its immediacy is represented through the lack of section titles that divide the other books of the work. Previously, titles set the parameters of Jane's memory, naming the experience she is narrating in terms of an event ("Freedom"), a philosophy ("Man's Way"), a vision ("The Chariot of Hell"), or a person ("Miss Lilly"). Such naming cannot be made for the action in "The Quarters," for it is not as far removed from Jane's present as the other sections, and as such, lacks the distance needed to construct a clear defining perspective. The section leaves the reader feeling that it will be the task of another oral historian to look back on its events from the vantage point of the future and give names to those sections which represent Jane's immediate past.

As Jane's autobiography comes forward in time and prepares to address issues that will reverberate in the future, a theme that Gaines will explore in his last two novels emerges: the nature of leadership. Jane and the people of her community are desperately seeking "the One," a Moses to lead them out of economic and psychological bondage. As Jane describes the community in this portion of her narrative, it consists of people searching for dignity even if they must settle for the vicarious esteem derived from the exploits of black athletes. By following such figures as Joe Louis or Jackie Robinson, Jane and her community experience an affirmation their society denies them:

When times get really hard, really tough, He always send you somebody. In the Depression . . . He sent us Joe. Joe was to lift the colored people's heart. . . . I heard every lick of that fight on the radio, and what Joe didn't put on S'mellin' that night just couldn't go on a man. . . .

Now, after the war, He sent us Jackie. . . . He showed them a trick or two. Homeruns, steal bases—eh Lord. It made my day just to hear what Jackie had done. (*MJP*, 201–2)

In their own ways, Louis and Robinson are leaders, and in her own way, Jane will become a leader as well.

The communal wish for a figure to do within their parish what Joe Louis and Jackie Robinson have done before the world manifests itself in close examination of each youth in the quarters, to see whether any possesses the

qualities that make him or her "the One." At first the people's hope rests in
Ned, but the certainty of Ned's martyrdom is expressed through Jane's
statement "Both of us knowed that day was coming. When and where we
didn't know" (*MJP*, 114). When Ned is assassinated, the community must
renew its search for "the One." It spends many years waiting and searching,
but at long last a possible candidate appears. This time it is Jimmy Aaron,
and the community's desperation is reflected in Jane's explanation of why
Jimmy was chosen: "People's always looking for somebody to come lead
them. . . . Anytime a child is born, the old people look in his face and ask
him if he's the One. . . . Why did we pick him? Well, why do you pick anybody? We picked him because we needed somebody" (*MJP*, 197–98).

As a youth, Jimmy feels summoned to a cause he cannot yet articulate.
As Jane describes him, "Jimmy would be sitting there on the gallery talking, and all a sudden he would stop listening to what I was saying and start
gazing out in the road like he was listening to something else. One day . . .
[h]e said, 'Miss Jane, I got something like a tiger in my chest, just gnawing
and . . . want come out. . . . I pray to God to take it out, but look like the
Lord don't hear me'" (*MJP*, 213). The image of an indifferent God crystallizes Jimmy's realization that man, he in particular, must do something to
rid himself of the "gnawing" and help his people. Like Ned, he too goes
away to be educated, and returns as an active participant in the civil rights
movement. And like Ned before him, Jimmy seeks to vanquish racial
injustice through peaceful protests modeled after those of Martin Luther
King, Jr.

Ned and Jimmy are descendants of characters found in Gaines's earlier
fiction: Copper Laurent in *Bloodline,* who in spite of his biracial heritage attempts to reclaim his family legacy; Jackson Bradley in *Catherine Carmier,*
who through loving the Creole Catherine seeks to move outside the boundaries set for him by his society; and Marcus in *Of Love and Dust,* who wants
to be more than "just a slave." What all these characters share, in addition to
a common determination to go against the status quo, is a common failure.
None have a lasting impact, and for the most part, the systems they confront remain unchanged. Through their failure Gaines implies that the
monolith of racism cannot be easily demolished. Razing it will necessitate a
different kind of tactic, a different kind of courage, a different kind of
leadership.

Ultimately at the end of the autobiography, it is Jane who emerges as a
true leader and effects change, not through rhetoric, or as she terms it "retrick,"[12] not through tactics, but through her sheer presence and the symbolism embodied in her life. Her decision to go to Bayonne and carry on the

protest begun by Jimmy (actually, in a larger context begun by Ned) is the catalyst that charges the rest of the community. A full circle is completed here, as the novel begins with Jane in a position of leadership, guiding Ned to Ohio and freedom, and ends with Jane in a similar position, leading her people in peaceful protest.

Jane's confrontation with racism is not one bordering on insanity, as is Copper's; it is not one that lacks direction, as does Jackson's; and it is not one that is destined to fail from the beginning, as is Marcus's. Gaines casts it as a simple act of personal dignity that commands respect, and the very simplicity of its nature seems to guarantee its success. When Robert Samson, the owner of her plantation, attempts to stop her from attending the protest in Bayonne by reminding her of Jimmy's death, Jane replies, "Just a little piece of him is dead. . . . The rest of him is waiting for us in Bayonne" (*MJP,* 244). She ends her autobiography by describing a scene of quiet strength and understated defiance as she closes: "Me and Robert looked at each other there a long time, then I went by him" (*MJP,* 244). The introductory clause of this sentence is a relatively long one for the phraseology given Jane Pittman and serves to build the suspense that allows us to appreciate the finality of Jane's action in the second clause, "then I went by him."

As Gaines considers the question of leadership, it is evident that for him any real and lasting change must be effected through leaders and actions firmly rooted in a cultural past. What makes Jane such a symbol to her people is her connection to the African-American past and her embodiment of African-American history. The people of the quarters look at Jane and see not a leader in the traditional sense of the word but a woman who has lived 111 years, one whose life has spanned many of the major events of black American history. In Jane they can see themselves, their parents, their grandparents, and their great-grandparents. Her presence personalizes their ancestral and sociopolitical history, while giving them strength to form a positive future.

Paraphrasing William Faulkner, Gaines has often stated, "The past ain't dead; it ain't even passed." *Miss Jane* reminds us that the past is never a distant memory for Ernest Gaines but is instead a constant influence on the present and future. As he listened to the stories of the old folks on his Aunt Augusteen's porch, the past arose, lived again, and donned a mantle of immediacy, and this influence of living cultural repositories was not lost on him. Accounts of what went before shape his creation of present literary experience, and homage to the past is characteristic, leading him to say of his work, "I was writing in a definite pattern. . . . I was going farther and farther back into the past. I was trying to go back, back, back into our experi-

ences in this country to find some kind of meaning to our present lives"
("MJ and I," 34). It is this meaning that Gaines embodies in Jane, and it
this meaning that empowers her story to complement traditional histories.
She recalls her life and that of others with a clarity that fosters an appreciation of the importance of her people's history to American culture. Jane's
autobiography is an American history amplified by the many strains of
African-American culture that conventional histories of the United States
may have muted. Her fictional narrative becomes a timeless American epic
as myth, religion, and the recollections of former slaves all accentuate the
historicity of her tale and Gaines's vision.

While the actions, patterns, and motifs of the novel are compelling and
create a riveting history of America from slavery to the mid-1960s, it is Miss
Jane whom we remember. She is the composite of all Gaines characters who
embark upon difficult journeys leading to psychic freedom and definitions
of self contrary to those their society imposes upon them.

Chapter Six

Identity and Integrity in
In My Father's House

You must stand individually . . . to stand with the crowd.
—Ernest Gaines

Past and present interact constantly in the fiction of Ernest Gaines as characters try to reconcile knowledge of the past with their present existence. Being aware of and at ease with the past is vital to understanding the present and surviving in the future. What makes Jane Pittman the leader her people so desperately seek is her embodiment of folk history. In his second-to-last novel Gaines continues probing the relationship of past reconcilement and future leadership touched upon in Jane's saga. Through the character Phillip Martin, he examines the relationship between past knowledge, present experience, and future leadership.

When *In My Father's House* opens, the Reverend Phillip Martin is a respected minister and civil rights leader. He is reminiscent of the Reverend Martin Luther King, Jr., as the allusion in his name implies, and Phillip has a long, successful history of nonviolent civil rights protests. The community he has piloted is now in transition, however, and its younger members, many of them teachers, are disillusioned with his approach to effecting change. They, like earlier Gaines characters, such as Jackson Bradley and Jimmy Aaron, possess a cynicism resulting from their education, and they no longer have faith in the leadership of Phillip Martin and older, church-oriented members of the grass-roots movement.

To weather generational divisiveness and enact fundamental changes that will secure his community's future, Phillip needs uncommon forbearance, and for inspiration he draws upon his memory of the successful protests he has mounted. Recalling past triumphs strengthens his resolve, but at this crucial crossroads Phillip is forced to confront a less pleasant memory. While he struggles to maintain his stature of community leader by generating enthusiasm for an economic boycott, Phillip must also struggle with a portion of the past he has denied, the son he deserted, Robert X.

The arrival of Robert X is shrouded in mystery. His cryptic presence is implied by the unknown variable he takes for his surname, a ritual practiced by the Black Muslims who follow Elijah Muhammad. Refusing to keep the names given to their ancestors by slaveholders but having no knowledge as to what names should properly replace them, the Black Muslims employ the letter X as a constant reminder of the uncertainty of familial identity bred by slavery. The Black Muslims believe that to accept the family names given by enslavers is also to accept an identity embodying dehumanization and debasement.[1] The severing of familial ties exemplified in the Black Muslim naming tradition becomes a fitting symbol for Gaines as he addresses what he acknowledges is a constant motif, the search of sons for fathers: "In my books there always seem to be fathers and sons searching for each other. That's a theme I've worked with since I started writing. Even when the father was not in the story. I've dealt with his absence and its effects on his children" (Desruisseaux, 13). Whether it is Copper Laurent or Robert X seeking to rightfully be acknowledged, the psychic state of Gaines's male characters is a direct result of paternal presence or absence. The effect of Phillip's desertion on Robert, together with Robert's subsequent decision to force Phillip into a realization of the consequences of his past actions, creates an arena for the interaction of past and present within the novel. Paternal lineage evolves into a symbol of continuity representing the search for past meaning to make sense of present existence.

Robert searches for familial continuity as represented through the ideal of a father. In keeping with the distance he perceives between his self-awareness and his given name, he calls himself Robert, which is not his true name; drops his surname; and adopts the unknown quantity. As Phillip's firstborn, he keenly feels that the family name Martin should have defined his identity, but when Phillip's desertion forces a redefinition of his identity and his present existence, the name becomes meaningless and he assumes an alias. He knows who his father is, but Phillip's abandonment and the subsequent family tragedy to which it leads create a past that Robert cannot accept, a past that emasculates and dehumanizes him. Since Phillip provides him with no true familial identification, to maintain his name would be to perpetuate a past that he sees as a hoax and desperately seeks to exorcise. Robert enters the novel as a mysterious presence with no history, no identity, and no epithet. For the majority of the work he remains nameless, referred to mostly as "Virginia's tenant."

With an X for his last name, Robert, like his father, becomes an allusion to a prominent political figure, one in sharp contrast to Martin Luther King. His name suggests Malcolm X, and about Malcolm, Gaines says the following: "Some critics have said that this is one of the things that Malcolm could have taught us that you go through hell but come out a whole man. I think that I was trying to get some of that into my literature before I had read Malcolm" (Beauford, 17).[2] Unfortunately, Robert X is never given the opportunity to attain the regenerative wholeness Gaines sees represented in Malcolm X; instead, he remains psychically fragmented, ultimately taking his own life. The conjuring of Martin Luther King and Malcolm X is further appropriate to Gaines's theme because the two can be viewed as a symbolic father-son representing generational differences in the civil rights movement and the many generational conflicts in the novel.

The extremes epitomized by Phillip and Robert are foreshadowed early in the novel through their vastly different introductions. Virginia Colar is the owner of the boardinghouse Robert selects as his residence when he arrives in the small city of St. Adrienne in search of Phillip. A sensitive and perceptive woman, Virginia is filled with foreboding by Robert's aspect, and she describes him in the following manner: "She didn't like his looks. He was too thin, too hungry-looking. She didn't like the little twisted knots of hair on his face that passed for a beard. He looked sick. His jaws were too sunken-in for someone his age. His deep-set bloodshot eyes wandered too much. . . . He definitely looked like somebody who had been shut in."[3] Robert's introductory description differs sharply from that given of his father: "Phillip Martin wore a black pinstriped suit, a light gray shirt, and a red polka-dot tie. He was sixty years old, just over six feet tall, and he weighed around two hundred pounds. His thick black hair and thick well-trimmed mustache were just beginning to show some gray. Phillip was a very handsome dark-brown-skinned man, admired by women, black and white. . . . He was very much respected by most of the people who knew him" (*FH*, 34). Phillip possesses a vitality that Robert does not. He enjoys an anchored position in his community, as evidenced by the name of the church of which he is pastor, the Solid Rock Baptist Church. The legacy he bequeaths Robert, however, is one of instability that renders Robert an outcast, tormented by a past lacking the identification a paternal lineage represents. Robert's psychic fragmentation causes him to return to St. Adrienne and aimlessly walk the street. His rambling brings him into contact with others, and his pitiable, silent presence forces their self-examination and in Phillip's case forces the exposure of self-deception. The juxtapositioning of this father and son establishes the larger thematic antagonisms of the story: youth and age, conservatism and radicalism, known and unknown, urban and rural, private and public, and most importantly, past and present. Through these oppositions Gaines makes a broader statement about the relationship between past and present, identity and integrity. If the significance of *The Autobiography of Miss Jane Pittman* is that knowledge of the past is vital to shaping future action, then the significance of *In My Father's House* is that *acknowledgment* of the past is integral to ensuring future meaning.

In My Father's House represents a departure from many of Gaines's trademarks. The tradition of oral storytelling, the setting of the plantation, and the use of voice that play such vital roles in the rest of his canon are modulated here. He is less concerned with realistically re-creating a time, a place, or a memorial to a particular cultural past than he is with exploring a concept with many general implications, the relationship of past and present as both affect identity. The lush naturalistic images of Louisiana found in *Catherine Carmier* are replaced by extensive descriptions of internal psychological terrain. First-person narratives are replaced by an omniscient narrative because Gaines feels it is the only appropriate voice for Phillip's story: "[C]ertain books require that you write not from the first person but from the omniscient point of view. *In My Father's House* is just such a book. You cannot tell that story from the minister's point of view because the minister keeps too much inside him. He does not reveal it—he won't reveal it to anybody. . . . So the story has to be told from that omniscient point of view" (Rowell, 41–42).

Continuing to probe the relationship of leadership and individual identity as he did in *The Autobiography of Miss Jane Pittman,* and returning to the quest motif of *Bloodline,* Gaines investigates the past's role in the creation of character, while at the same time exploring the relationship of a father and his son. Phillip Martin is a leader, but the novel seems to query how a man who 22 years earlier forsook the role of leadership within his own family can accept the mantle of leadership in the present. Throughout the work, Phillip must reevaluate social conscience in light of personal conscience, and he undertakes a journey that obliges him to recognize his past in order to salvage his future.

The impetus for Phillip's odyssey begins in his living room as members of the black community gather to debate the effectiveness of various strategies of protest. Primarily they are considering the necessity of white participation to the success of their movement for civil rights. At this point Phillip is a conciliating force, harmonizing the polar factions of the progressive and conservative elements in the community. His placidity is upset, however, when in the midst of the gathering he sees his eldest son. He does not completely remember him, but an intuitive shock of recognition leaves him paralyzed. His inability to act and his inability to acknowledge Robert lay the foundation for the collapse of his power as a black leader, and the eventual erosion of his influence is depicted through his needing physical support from the two whites present at the gathering:

> He looked puzzled, confused, a deep furrow came into his forehead, and he raised his hand up to his temple as if he were in pain. . . . He pushed his way out of the crowd and started across the room. He had taken only two or three steps when he suddenly staggered and fell heavily to the floor.
>
> The pharmacist, Octave Bacheron . . . knelt on the other side of him, put his small white hand on Phillip's chest and told him to lie still a moment. . . . Octave Bacheron nodded to Anthony to help him get Phillip to his feet. . . . Phillip told them again that he was all right and he could stand on his own. But the two white men insisted on helping him to his feet, and they made him lean on them. (*FH,* 39–42).

The image of the fallen civil rights leader, now propped by two white men, vividly conveys Phillip's diminished stature as a leader and sets the stage for the depiction of his diminished stature as a father, and hence as a man. His collapse in his living room starts him on a journey to his past and subsequently to the acknowledgment of those aspects of his identity he has denied. The voyage through his history is an arduous one and begins with deep introspection within the darkened quiet of his study, where he goes for solace after his encounter with Robert.

Phillip's study reflects the values that have formed the nucleus of his political philosophy. His integrationist ideology is symbolized in the pastiches that decorate the walls of his office: "On the left was a collage of President John Kennedy, Robert Kennedy, and Martin Luther King. In another frame hanging evenly with the first was another collage of Abraham Lincoln, Frederick Douglass, and Booker T. Washington" (*FH,* 52). In the content of the two pictures an evolution from past to present is evident. It is also interesting to note that King, like Phillip in the earlier scene in his living room, is in the presence of two whites who seek to contribute to the cause of civil rights. When contrasted to the collage in which two early black leaders, Douglass and Washington, are joined with Lincoln, the pastiche of later figures might imply a dilution of black power caused by an increasing white presence and signify the dilution more radical members within Phillip's organization fear.

For Phillip, however, the collages and their placement have no negative meaning or import. They reflect both his belief in the power of integration and his belief that a society representing an amalgam of distinct races ensures progress for all. To him they evoke a sense of timelessness, as those who worked for racial coexistence in the past are poised with those who work for it in the present. As they hang "evenly" in his study, they indicate no tension between past and present and are representations of the steady progression Phillip has enjoyed while forging his public identity. The symbolic harmony of past and present contained in his choice of collages is not displayed in his own life, however, and the continuity of his identity is now threatened by Robert's presence. He has acknowledged his political history and its place in his public present, but he must now acknowledge his personal history and its place in his private future.

It falls to Phillip to reexamine his motives and values and attempt to reconnect with his past, just as he must reconnect with his son. He has denied his personal history by running from it and has run so far that reconstruction of his prior life becomes difficult. As he endeavors to recall the details of the family he deserted, he cannot, and even the most important and concrete details surrounding them, in particular the details of his eldest son, remain nebulous: "He had been sitting there the last few minutes thinking about his son. He knew Robert was not his name. And he had been sitting there trying to think of his true name" (*FH*, 62). Forgetting his son's name indicates the great effort Phillip has expended in divorcing his present identity from the actions of his past. But as Robert's appearance reminds him, the present is a consequence of the past and the past will aways be a specter.

The increasing self-examination forced by the apparition of his prior life makes Phillip aware of the "two" Phillip Martins. The collision of conflicting identities torments him until he commits a desperate and selfish act. When Robert is arrested for vagrancy, Phillip's guilt compels him to bail him out and compromise the integrity not only of his position as a leader but also of the upcoming protest his community plans. His attempt to redress the wrongs he committed prior to becoming a minister leads him to enter into questionable negotiation with the town's sheriff, Nolan, and new transgressions compound the old.

Nolan's and Martin's social roles have placed them at ideological odds with each other, but in spite of their opposing positions, Nolan holds a grudging respect for what Phillip has stood for and what he has accomplished. Phillip sullies this respect, however, when he enters into a pact in which Nolan agrees to free Robert from jail and keep the secret of his paternity. In return, Phillip contracts to restrain his community from launching the demonstration they had planned. This new secret solves nothing and only obscures Phillip's route to his sense of self. He pays a high price for his guilt—a loss of self-respect and the loss of his position as leader. Even

Nolan says at the close of their dealings, in reference to both Phillip's compromising and his desertion, "I always thought you was different. . . . Just go to show how wrong a man can be" (*FH*, 92). Phillip's diminished prestige is accompanied by a diminished self-esteem, and both are manifested through a loss of standing in the community. His followers view him as having bargained with the devil, and disempower him, for no one person's interests can be greater than those of the larger community's. As one member of the committee organizing the upcoming protest tells Phillip, "I want [my son] . . . out of that jail right now. But I know I don't have no right to ask the people to sacrifice everything for him. No one person can come before the cause, Reverend. Not even you" (*FH*, 122). Ironically, his community's stripping him of his public identity frees Phillip to pursue a private identity imprisoned in the past.

Phillip's divorce from his people isolates him, and his detachment is represented through the running image of a solitary pecan tree. Upon first describing the tree he refers to it as "leafless," indicating his own barrenness, as he now stands rooted in the community but lacking the branches and leaves that represent familial extensions to his son, Robert. Later, after he is unable to tell his present wife, Alma; his friends; or his associates about Robert, he describes the pecan tree in a manner that indicates the seclusion and social coldness he feels while singly bearing the secret of his son: "The lawn was white with frost. The pecan tree in the open pasture across the street stood bare and alone" (*FH*, 68). To rejoin the fold of family and community, Phillip must find a way of making his past consistent with his present.

His first step in reconciling his opposing personas is to stop running from his former existence. Every decision he has made in his life was made in the shadow of his past, even his decision to choose the ministry as a vocation. As he tells an old friend, "I went to religion to forget it. I prayed and prayed and prayed to forget it. I tried to wipe out everything in my past, make my mind blank, start all over. I thought the good work I was doing with the church, with the people, would make up for all the things I had done in the past. Till one day I looked cross my living room. . . . From the moment I saw him in that house—I fell . . . I fell" (*FH*, 201). Phillip's attempts to redeem past transgressions through virtue and contrition dissipate with the advent of his son. The memory of his desertion will not allow him to find comfort in his deeds, and Robert does not allow him to exonerate himself through his religion.

Robert reminds his father that no amount of sorrow, regret, or religious purging can atone for the abandonment of family and disavowal of personal history. His mordant comments bitterly point out the irony of a man who has destroyed the souls of his family now making his lifework the saving of souls: "The man told Mama . . . you had found God, and you was down here saving souls. Mama thought it was the funniest thing she ever heard. . . . After you had destroyed us, you down here saving souls" (*FH*, 100). Robert's revelation of the hypocrisy inherent in Phillip's conception of himself renders hollow any rationale Phillip might offer, but Phillip does offer an apology for himself, and ironically he turns to the past—the larger African-American cultural past, that is—to assist him.

As he examines his conscience, Phillip is powerless to find personal extenuation. Because he can conceive of no circumstances in his life adequate to absolve him of his guilt, he attempts to construct a historical explanation for his actions. As he speaks to Robert, he endeavors to create a context for his behavior, but the emptiness of his explanations becomes obvious and serves only to accentuate Phillip's lack of responsibility more conspicuously: "I had a mouth, but I didn't have a voice. . . . I had arms, but I couldn't lift them up to you. It took a man to do these things, and I wasn't a man. I was just some other brutish animal who could cheat, steal, rob, kill—but not stand. Not be responsible. Not protect you or your mother. They had branded that in us from the time of slavery" (*FH*, 102). It is too convenient for Phillip, a man who runs from his past, to seek refuge in his people's cultural past to justify his selfish actions. His rationale ironically becomes, to borrow Sartre's terminology, "bad faith" as insincere as that of earlier Gaines characters who use history to justify their moral wrongs. Remembering the explanation given by the uncle in the short story "Bloodline," Frank Laurent, who denies his nephew, Copper, his legacy because of his black heritage, we remember a white man who blames history for racial wrongs and insists that because he is merely one man, a victim of a monolithic system impervious to transformation, he cannot effect change. Phillip's apology is similar, as he joins the characters who prefer the path of least personal accountability, using history to justify the mistakes of individuals. The conception of history that Phillip relies upon in formulating excuses is in sharp contrast to the vision of history generally expressed in Gaines's canon. For Phillip, it is not the vivid, personal, oral history that such characters as Jane Pittman use to actualize themselves; it is an empty justifier, an abstract concept used to shift personal responsibility for actions from "I" to "they."

Phillip's fragile self-image is based on illusion. To strengthen his conception of himself, he must rediscover the elements that compose his identity. His first step in his unearthing of self is to realize he can offer no adequate explanation for his actions and to cease running from his past. Since he can imagine no way to reconnect with the events that have made him the man he is, other than actually to seek out those people who have knowledge of him in another time, gropingly, awkwardly, and with no clear plan he returns to the Reno plantation where he grew up. This is the only portion of the novel that unfolds in the rural setting omnipresent in Gaines's other works. Using this site as the locale for Phillip's regeneration implies that his truth cannot be found in the urban community in which he now lives but must instead be sought in his rural parish with the communal memory that connects him to the past. Appropriately, the information guiding him to sources that aid in self-reconciliation comes from a figure we have seen in many of Gaines's works in the persons of Aunt Clo, Aunt Fe, and Jane Pittman. Each of these women is an icon of the past, and Phillip's godmother, Angelina Bouie, is modeled in the same fashion. She is oracle, guiding him to knowledge of his personal history.

As Phillip returns to the house of his "nanane," he returns to a world more familiar to Gaines's readers than the city of St. Adrienne. The quarters of Reno plantation are peopled with characters resembling those in *Catherine Carmier* and *Of Love and Dust*. Just as Madame Bayonne can see the soul of Jackson Bradley in his eyes, and just as Jim Kelly can see Marcus's defiance in his aspect, so too can Phillip's godmother, a "small, very old woman," regard him and know "there was something wrong in St. Adrienne" (*FH,* 111). She gives him sympathy, but more importantly, she gives him the intelligence that tells him where his journey to his past should begin. Angelina informs Phillip that his boyhood friend, Chippo Simon, has seen Robert's mother, Johanna. Because he believes Chippo might be able to furnish him with the information he seeks, Phillip becomes obsessed with finding Chippo. Looking for his former consort takes him back to the parish where he grew up, and each person he encounters serves to move him further from his present identity as minister and leader, and closer to his past.

His first significant encounter is with a self-styled "reverend," the Reverend Peters, a man in his seventies or eighties whose appearance reflects Phillip's perception of himself after his "fall": "The man looked very tired, his eyes watery and bloodshot" (*FH,* 151). In the aged man's weary aspect and in the sham of spiritual leadership he proffers, Phillip sees a manifestion of a psychological existence too close to his own. No longer is he "Reverend Martin," a genuine man of the cloth; he is now a pretender, a parody of a religious symbol. The more Phillip's self-contempt increases, the more he sees himself in Peters. In one instance when he can no longer abide the homilies Peters offers, Phillip equates Peters's ineffectual religious platitudes with his own teachings. Peters attempts to instill in Phillip belief in future success,

but Phillip paradoxically adopts the cynicism of the younger members of his
own congregation. In response to Reverend Peters's soothing remarks that
all will work out "if you have faith," Phillip's reply, "There's a gap between
us and our sons . . . that even He . . . can't seem to close" (*FH*, 154), dis-
misses as a simple placebo the faith he has spent his life encouraging. His
harsh confrontation with personal truth has rendered him unable to believe
in the machinations of a larger deity and has further distanced him from his
calling as spiritual leader. The further Phillip moves from his identity as religious leader and upright citizen, the closer he comes to a coexistence with
those very elements in his community from which he was so removed.

A second encounter with a young man of Robert's age, Billy, moves
Phillip closer to an understanding of his son's anger. The relationship that
Billy and his father share strikes a chord of cognizance in Phillip, and he
uses Billy as a sounding board while he gropes to find the words that can explain his actions to his own son. Billy does not reveal the sympathy for fathers that Phillip hopes to find; instead, he tells Phillip, "My daddy got to
catch up with me. . . . I can't go back where he's at" (*FH*, 166), and makes
Phillip realize that as a father, he must be responsible for reconstructing the
bond with his son. Phillip is at a loss as to how to do so, however, and seeks
guidance from Billy:

"How do we close the gap, Billy?". . .
    "I don't know," Billy said.
    "The church?"
    "Shit," Billy said, without hesitating a moment. "There ain't nothing in them
churches, Pops, but more separation. Every little church got they own little crowd,
like gangs out on the street. They all got to outdo the other one. Don't look for that
crowd to close no gap."
    "The whole civil rights program started in the church."
    "Just because I can eat at the white folks' counter with my daddy, just because
I can ride side him in the front of the bus don't mean we any closer," Billy said.
    (*FH*, 166)

In a single conversation Billy undercuts the two most important aspects of
Phillip's identity, his role as a minister and his role as a civil rights leader.
Billy's assessment renders both roles futile and intimates that more than political activism or religious ritual is needed to close the fissure between fathers and sons. His comments reiterate the novel's theme that personal
bonds must be secure before social ones can be formed.

In looking at the rupture between Billy and his father, Phillip sees himself and Robert, and by extension, his generation and the next. His realization forces a reevaluation of his role as a religious and political leader, evident in subsequent reflections: "He was still thinking about Billy, comparing him to his own son in St. Adrienne. They were about the same age, and they were saying practically the same thing. There were probably many others just like them. He saw it in some of the younger schoolteachers in St. Adrienne. They could not say in public the things that Billy and his son could say, but by their actions they showed that they felt the same way about God, Law, and Country. He asked himself how would he ever reach them—could he ever reach them?" (*FH*, 170). Phillip's despair over the gaping breach between him and Robert echoes Gaines's own pondering as to how the chasm between fathers and sons can be closed: "I don't know what it will take to bring them together again. I don't know that the Christian religion will bring fathers and sons together again. I don't know that the father will ever be in a position—a political position or any position of authority—from which he can reach out and bring his son back to him again" (Rowell, 40).

As Gaines alludes to the position of authority and political power from which a black father might regain his son, he evokes Phillip's situation as minister, leader, and father. Even from his social vantage point, Phillip cannot reach Robert and continues a process of soul-searching to discover what obstacles prevent him from doing so. In his retrospection, every question Phillip ponders in relation to his public identity has a direct impact on his private one. By examining his ability to lead the young, for example, he is actually querying his identity as a father and family leader. His continuing self-scrutiny makes his awareness of a dual existence even more acute, and a veil of remorse obscures the minister in St. Adrienne from the view of the man in Reno plantation.

Paralleling Phillip's movement away from his St. Adrienne identity is a movement toward persons farther in his past, those more closely affiliated with the existence he sought to escape. In his pursuit of Chippo, he finds himself searching bars and gambling houses, places that worship far-different ideals from those worshiped in the Solid Rock Baptist Church. From the self-styled Reverend Peters to Billy and now to a former flame, Adeline Toussaint, Phillip has followed a downward spiral from minister to father to carnal man. Adeline reminds Phillip of the side of him he wants to forget, and seeing her brings back desires he would rather disregard, but cannot, as he notices, "She was a very handsome woman, with high cheekbones, large dark-brown eyes, and full lips. . . . She and Phillip had been lovers once. A sudden warm good feeling came over him that he wished was not there" (*FH*, 174). He feels a passion for Adeline that he does not feel for his wife, Alma, a passion that reminds him of his life "before religion." His conversation with her contributes another dimension to his self-understanding, and for a moment he experiences the hurt selfish acts of desire can cause when Adeline hints that she may have pretended a love that was not there:

"But you did love once?"
    "Did I?"
    "You said so."
    She laughed. "Stop it, Phillip Martin."
    He was hurt. "Well?"
    "How many times that's been said by both man and woman? How many times you yourself have said that to a woman? You meant it every time?" (*FH*, 177)

Adeline's responses force Phillip into a position similar to the one he has placed women in but has seldom been placed in himself. Her confession to an innocuous duplicity magnifies the more tragic consequences of his own duplicity as he denied his past to live in the illusion of his present.

Phillip's encounter with Reverend Peters forces him to evaluate his validity as a minister; his conversation with Billy compels him to acknowledge the irrelevancy of his religious and political ideologies to an upcoming generation; and his meeting with Adeline forces him to admit to the guile that governed his relationships with women. None of these realizations have been easy for Phillip, but the most difficult encounter, his encounter with Chippo, still awaits him. Fatigued from his burden of self-truths, he tells Adeline, "I'm very tired. But I have to find Chippo" (*FH*, 178), and resolves to uncover the final key to his past.

The Phillip that ultimately does see Chippo is a very different one from the minister and civil rights leader in the beginning of the novel. He is a Phillip who remembers that Robert "was not his only child out of wedlock. He had children that he knew of by three or four other women. And he had been as proud of it as any other man" (*FH*, 150). He is a Phillip who recalls the following experience: "Talking to a newspaper man—a man who's covered executions all over the South. . . . Most of them, black men. Said he never heard one called Daddy's name at that last hour. Heard mama called, gran'mon, nanane—Jesus, God. Not one time he heard daddy called" (*FH*, 153). He is a Phillip who, looking at Chippo "with bloodshot eyes . . . tired and worried" (*FH*, 181), is closer in appearance to the opening physical description of his son, Robert X.

Chippo Simon is Phillip's alter ego. He is the embodiment of the desires Phillip has kept hidden, the other side of Phillip's public personality, what Phillip would be had he not found religion: a "tall, slim, but solidly built man in his early sixties. His long, narrow face was the color of dark, well-used leather, and it looked just as tough. . . . He looked like a person who did not worry much; he would take life as it came" (*FH,* 180). Chippo has dissipated himself with liquor, women, and bad debts, and in the course of his life has come upon the truths Phillip needs to unify his two identities. It is Chippo who can tell Phillip the true name of Robert X, Etienne, and the name of his other two children by Johanna, Antoine and Justine. It is also Chippo who can tell him of his other family's tragedy and his eldest son's psychological disintegration. Chippo reveals to Phillip that Robert's ranging began prior to his arrival at St. Adrienne and that in seeking his father he seeks an unformed retribution: "At night he went out walking. The people saw him. Then back to the house—to the room—laying there woke, listening, waiting. Waiting. Waiting. Waiting for what? Another chance? He had failed his sister. What was he waiting for—to defend mama? That's why he lay there waiting? What other reason?" (*FH,* 199). Chippo's revelation of the fate of Phillip's family is a weighty one, and "where Chippo's mind had been relieved of a burden by talking about it, Phillip now felt a heavier burden by hearing it" (*FH,* 200). The saga causes an implosion of thought in Phillip's mind. He retraces his life, particularly the recent events that led to this point, and realizes he is as powerless to reach Robert now as he was when he first encountered him in his living room. When Alma, Phillip's wife, and Shepherd, one of the teachers in Phillip's congregation, arrive at Chippo's after searching for Phillip with the news of the fate that has befallen Robert, Phillip's implosion of thought turns into an explosion of frustrated violence. He takes random blows at Chippo, at Shepherd, then turns from them, "looking for something to hit, something to break. But there was nothing near him. The walls were too far for him to reach" (*FH,* 207). Wishing to strike out at his past to eradicate it, he cannot. Like the walls that surround him, it is "too far for him to reach."

Phillip cannot make amends for the past but must find a way to place it in a new perspective. With the help of Chippo, who tells him, "You can't stop man. . . . We need you out there too much. . . . I need somebody to look up to" (*FH,* 208), he begins to revise his identity as man, minister, and leader. By articulating his need for someone to look up to, Chippo replaces the fallen Phillip in a position of leadership, but it is leadership encompassing a different meaning. As he exists for Chippo, Phillip is no longer a trailblazer whose effectiveness is intertwined with untarnished prominence. He is a leader because he has human frailties, can overcome these frailties, and can emerge as a stronger individual. Reconciling himself to Chippo's vision, Phillip reconnects himself to those he has forgotten and now has the potential to be a more appropriate leader, one firmly rooted in his past. Like Jane Pittman, by living example he can become an effectual guide.

Phillip's past victories are also placed in a different context when he realizes that his past identity is not separate from but an integral part of his present identity. Another teacher in the room, Beverly Ricord, helps Phillip see that all along, his running away from his past has constituted a tacit recognition of its existence and that this recognition has been the impetus motivating him to action for the good of all. Recalling his protest to gain his people access to the legal system, Beverly states, "There're many more people who walk up to that courthouse today without trembling. I go up there today without trembling. Shepherd go up there today without trembling. I take my class there, and they walk all through that courthouse without trembling. Your son Patrick is in my class. He's one of the proudest little boys you'll ever meet. Why? Because Daddy made all this possible" (*FH,* 212). Phillip's gaining tangible entry to the courthouse is now complemented by his gaining spiritual access to a new understanding of what he has done and why. No longer does he conceive of his achievements in large, abstract, and public terms; he now sees them as the very concrete improvements to daily black life that they are. Redefining his role as a leader moves him to a subsequent reconsideration of his role as a father. Though he has failed Robert and his other children, he has been a good father to his current family, and with Beverly's help Phillip can view Patrick as the reincarnation of his lost son, Robert. Through Patrick, Phillip has a chance to do what he could not do with his firstborn, construct a concrete father-son relationship.

Phillip's remarks to his wife, Alma, reveal a floundering man weary of introspection and at the beginning of another odyssey, this one not to rediscover the past but to discover the future:

> "I'm lost, Alma. I'm lost."
> "Shhh," she said. "Shhh. Shhh. We just go'n have to start again." (*FH,* 214)

Start again is what Phillip must do to create a new, more complete, and accurate identity.

The rifts between Phillip and Robert, between Billy and his father, between the younger members of the church and the older have a common cause, lack of faith in the past. For Ernest Gaines, belief in the self is important, but integral to such belief is acceptance of the past. He modifies the adage "A man who forgets his past is bound to repeat it" to "A man should not forget his past but be bound to it." Phillip cannot run from his past, for it defines him. Any subsequent structure he builds in his life—whether the structure of a new family or the structure of social leadership—must securely rest on his past. His odyssey toward personal responsibility strengthens his integrity, and he sees that social impact is meaningful only as long as it can be measured in terms of individual and familial benefit. More important than political strides are individuals secure in themselves making personal strides toward their own dignity and not willing, as was Phillip Martin, to compromise that dignity.

The journeys to self-esteem begun by the boys Sonny and James, continued by the young men Jackson and Marcus, and culminating in the epic life of Jane Pittman are all woven into Phillip's search for dignity. His manhood and the respect that comes with it can only be realized when he grasps that private responsibility must be the necessary precursor to social responsibility.

Chapter Seven

Action and Self-Realization in
A Gathering of Old Men

Damn what *you* think I'm supposed to be—I will be what I ought to be.
—Ernest Gaines

I've even heard Negroes say that maybe Hitler and Mussolini are all right; that maybe Stalin is all right. They did not say this out of any intellectual comprehension of the forces at work in the world, but because they felt that these men "did things.". . . There was in the back of their minds, when they said this, a wild and intense longing (wild and intense because it was suppressed!) to belong, to be identified, to feel that they were alive as other people were, to be caught up forgetfully and exultingly in the swing of events, to feel the clean, deep, organic satisfaction of doing a job in common with others.[1]

In the suffocating racial and economic environment that serves as the setting for Richard Wright's novel *Native Son,* it takes an extreme act of brutal violence to provide the young hero, Bigger Thomas, with the opportunity to "do things." When he accidentally suffocates Mary Dalton, his wealthy white employer's daughter, then intentionally mutilates her body, for the first time in his life he feels he exists, that he is a force impacting on his environment, rather than a victim of its forces. Even though Bigger's motivation for killing Mary is a straightforward one—the fear of being a black man caught in the bedroom of a white woman—as he covers up his crime, the accident becomes an act of creation:

The thought of what he had done, the awful horror of it, the daring associated with such actions, formed for him for the first time in his fear-ridden life a barrier of protection between him and a world he feared. He had murdered and had created a new life for himself. It was something that was all his own, and it was the first time in his life he had had anything that others could not take from him. . . . Though he had killed by accident, not once did he feel the need to tell himself that it had been an accident. (Wright, 101)

Dismembering Mary and placing her in the furnace, creating the ransom note that implicates the Communist Jan, and plotting his escape all become Bigger's way of making an unintentional death an act for which he is responsible.[2] In this manner, he transforms a brutal action into the self-affirmation his society has denied him and finally feels he is a man.

The power to act, "to be identified," "to be caught up forgetfully and exultingly in the swing of events" is central to Gaines's final novel, *A Gathering of Old Men*, originally titled "The Revenge of Old Men." In this text, too, action is power. Men who for many years have waited as silent brutes at long last discard their yokes and seize power over their lives. They become men who "do things," and in a single act of courage reaffirm their manhood and humanity. Having tacitly supported a social order that relegated them to a subhuman existence, in their twilight years they realize the opportunity an act of murder provides them to salvage their dignity.

The old men reside in and around Marshall Quarters. Although the action takes place in the 1970s, social conventions change so slowly in Marshall that the novel could have taken place anytime during the period of tenant farming. Marshall is the remnant of a plantation in which "[T]here were nothing but old people. . . . The young ones had all gone away."[3] Their exodus is caused by the same Cajun infringement Gaines delineates in other novels. Here again, the Cajuns overtake, in one character's words, "[T]he very same land we had worked, our people had worked, and our people's people had worked since the time of slavery" (*GM*, 43). Because the Cajuns have so thoroughly subjugated the blacks of Marshall plantation, it comes as a shock to this community when a Cajun overseer is shot by a black man. The entire populace is left wondering how, on a plantation where there are only old men too bound to a system to change it, such a murder could take place. Shock turns to perplexity when *all* the elderly black men of the plantation claim responsibility for the killing. Participating in a scheme devised by the young white overseer, Candy Marshall, these men have vowed to hide the identity of the true killer and execute their final act of pride and dignity, confessing to the shooting of Beau Boutan.

Though only one man has actually shot Beau, each black man in the work has committed the same murder at one point, in his heart, in his mind. While he is only one white man, Beau represents all the white men who have disdained their existence and all the injustices that have been heaped upon them their entire lives. To claim to be Beau's killer provides each man with the opportunity to gain revenge against a society that has abused him and told him he is worthless. The men successfully fool the officials enforcing the rules of their society and subsequently cause a revolution through confusion.

As Gaines vivifies the saga of a gathering of men in their later years lifting the subjugation imposed upon them, he gathers the many themes of his previous works—the importance of the past, cultural displacement, appeasement versus affirmation—and engages them here. He also employs the techniques of storytelling that have become Gaines trademarks, particularly the use of first-person narrative. Such phrases as "But listen to this now" and "Wait—hold it—let me tell you" remind us that Gaines uses the oral tradition in rendering this story as he has others. Rather than divide the text into formal chapters, Gaines divides the novel into 15 narrated segments, each unfolding or illuminating the action from a different perspective and voice. Presented in this manner, the novel allows us the opportunity to know the characters' consciousness intimately, and what clearly emerges is the dual consciousness of men who have existed in a world of silent acceptance while dreaming of a world of willful action.

The notion of dual consciousness becomes important, because all the characters have two identities, one for larger society and one for their own intimate community. Gaines emphasizes their duality by titling each narrative segment with the two names by which each character is known, his or her formal name and the name he or she is most commonly called. The formal name might be considered the "written" name. It belongs to the world of official documents, legal access, and civil rights. This is the world to which the black men of this work have consistently been denied entry. The land they have farmed for generations is being taken away from them; the killing of Beau Boutan threatens them with white vigilantism from which the law cannot protect them; and at every turn they are denied their dignity as men. As the novel's action progresses, the men come to demand the societal recognition passage to this world implies. The white characters are also hampered by their written names, which define them as part of a racist system and force them to live by antiquated values. Because of his family name, the owner of Marshall plantation must uphold a legacy of race and caste that no longer has meaning in his life; the youngest son of the Boutan clan must fight with his father to end the cycle of racial hatred and retribution their society associates with their family name; and even the extremist vigilantes desire revenge because they feel they must uphold the birthright of the label "white men."

By contrast, the informal name might be termed the "oral" name. It belongs to the world of everyday consciousness, the world of "talk," a world consisting of day-to-day reality. The name deriving from this world is in

keeping with one's history, one's characteristics, and one's essence and receives meaning only when imbued with knowledge of this world. More than
a nickname, it is a reflection of character. The values society assigns the
races—white and therefore worthy, black and therefore unworthy—are not
part of the oral name, an appellation that goes past race and portrays one's
more internal qualities. All the characters oscillate between their two appel-
lations as they seek a comfortable balance between social and personal identity. If we take as an example the experience of Robert Louis Stevenson
Banks, a.k.a. Chimley, it is evident that the aspirations implicit in his name
are negated by a society that denies the validity of his existence.

Chimley's experience illustrates the relationship between naming and intent. His written name is fashioned after one who works with the written
word, a poet, a creative voice that transforms life experiences into verses. His
is a naming of honor, since one able to change experience into expression is
highly valued, whether it be the poet, the artist, or the blues musician.
Chimley's naming might be seen to express the hope that he too will be able
to accomplish what Paul Laurence Dunbar in his poem "The Poet" called a
voicing of the "world's absorbing heat."[4] But Chimley's experience never
finds a poetic expression in keeping with the symbolism of his name, for a
society unwilling to accept his worth as a man will certainly ignore the import of his formal name.

"Chimley," the name he is commonly known by, is rooted in his community and culture. It is given potency only by an understanding of the tradition that has inspired it, and outside that tradition it loses its meaning and
becomes only a nickname. Recognizing this, Chimley desires that those outside his cultural world call him by a name with meaning appropriate to that
context. As the narrator of this segment, Matt, describes Chimley's response
to the denial of his right to name himself, it becomes evident that for
Chimley, what he is called is not as important as who makes the decision of
appellation: "Chimley was . . . smaller . . . and . . . blacker than me . . .
that's why we all called him Chimley. He didn't mind his friends calling
him Chimley, 'cause he knowed we didn't mean nothing. But he sure didn't
like them white folks calling him Chimley. He was always telling them that
his daddy had named him Robert Louis Stevenson Banks, not Chimley. But
all they did was laugh at him, and they went on calling him Chimley any-
how" (*GM*, 39–40). To acknowledge someone's desire to be called a certain
name is to recognize that person's wish to be perceived with respect. While
those rooted in his society and traditions use "Chimley" with no desire to
denigrate and are aware of its meaning within his culture, those outside his
world who refuse to honor his existence as a man employ it in a manner that

implies degradation. Chimley actively wants to name himself and thereby accord himself the dignity his society denies him. Naming is one avenue that might confer self-esteem, but as the end of the quotation tells us, such is not the case in Chimley's plantation world, where those who cannot perceive his dignity use his informal name to patronize him.

The respect Chimley seeks is sought by all the black men in the novel, and their narratives unfold a series of experiences illustrating the persistent denial of acceptance. In his review, Reynolds Price likens the novel to a morality play, and this analogy provides an instructive framework for viewing the text.[5] According to David Bevington, morality plays were generally "characterized primarily by the use of allegory to convey a moral lesson about religious or civil conduct, presented through the medium of abstractions or representative social characters."[6] With narrated allegories representing the history of black and white relations, each character in *Gathering* becomes a representation of the violence, subjugation, and mutual hatred and love that contributed to the pageant of complex race relations in rural Louisiana.

The opening narrative segment is presented through the voice of a child, George Eliot, Jr., a.k.a. Snookum. Its placement is appropriate in a novel whose underlying theme is the questioning of senseless racial hatred. It is the work's Book of Genesis, and Snookum is the innocent Adam who has not yet partaken of the fruit of racism. Too young to understand fully the origins of the hatred that grips his community, he fills his Edenic narrative with childhood preoccupations. The prose of this segment is characterized by the repetition and ingenuous make-believe that characterize childlike expression, as is evident in the following passage: "I shot out of there, . . . spanking my butt the way you spank your horse when you want him to run fast. . . . I yanked my horse around and . . . headed up the quarters. . . . I turned around and shot out of there, spanking my butt the way you spank a horse when you want that horse to run fast. . . . I just hollered names; running, spanking my butt and hollering names" (*GM*, 6–7). In his ensuing conversation with another character, Janice Robinson, a.k.a. Janey, Snookum's innocence contrasts sharply to her reaction, and their differing responses accentuate the ominous consequences of a black man killing a white:

"What Candy want with them down in the quarters?" she asked me.

"Something to do with Mathu and Beau. Beau laying on his back in Mathu's yard. And Mathu squatting there with that shotgun."

Janey's face changed quick. She was mad at first, now she was scared . . . and grabbed me in the collar.

"That shot I heard?" she said. "That shot I heard?"

"That hurt," I said. . . . "Y'all got any tea cakes or plarines [pralines] in there?" (*GM*, 8–9)

Snookum's narrative is followed by Janey's, and innocence is replaced by awareness of an upcoming racial crisis. Substituted for the repetition and make-believe of his voice are Janey's repeated pleas to Jesus and God to assist in stemming the potential tragedy: "Lord have mercy, Jesus, what now? Where do I turn? Go where first? . . . [C]all Mr. Lou and Miss Merle. I better make it Mr. Lou first. Lord, have mercy, keep me on my feet if it is thy holy will" (*GM*, 10). The desperation of Janie's entreaties foreshadows the serious impact Beau's killing will have on the community, and each of the ensuing narratives portrays a portion of the history that has led to the crisis.

Each segment gives information vital to understanding the larger unfolding pageant. Viewing the novel in its entirety, the 10 narratives of the black characters create a composite of racial injustice, and the 5 narrative sections of white characters reveal disbelief and at times begrudging respect for the action these men undertake. There is a transformation, sometimes subtle, sometimes obvious, in how the white characters of the novel perceive these men and their worth, one that matches the transformation Beau's killing effects in the black characters. Perspectives detailing action alternate with perspectives probing action, and a comparison of the narratives "Myrtle Bouchard aka Miss Merle" and "Louis Alfred Dimoulin aka Lou Dimes" illustrates this complementary relationship.

As with all the characters in the work, Lou Dimes, the newsman, has two identities. His first, indicated by his formal name, is that of a white man, one the parish expects will uphold its social rules; his second, however, represented by the name Lou, is that of an objective reporter often sympathetic to the cause of the elderly black men. His language reflects the photographic precision necessary to detached reporting. In his depiction of the sheriff who has come to investigate Beau's death, Lou's exact characterization reminds us that we are seeing the action through the eyes of a seasoned reporter:

When I looked over my shoulder, Mapes had already stopped out in front of the house. He was sitting on the passenger side of the black Ford Fairlane, one of his deputies driving. . . . He was about my height, six three, six four, but he outweighed me by a hundred pounds at least. He was in his late sixties. He wore a gray lightweight suit, a gray hat, white shirt, and a red tie. His deputy, who wore a beige suit and tie but no hat, got out on the other side. He seemed to be in his early twenties. He was about five eight, and weighed round a hundred and forty pounds. (*GM*, 63)

Lou's meticulous descriptions present the objective reality of the novel's action; however, because he is an outsider who did not grow up within the traditions of Marshall plantation, it falls to another character, Myrtle Bouchard, to reveal the emotional tension of the present circumstances.

Myrtle's narrative details the social hierarchy within the plantation. The title "Miss" given as part of her second name indicates her position as a member of the white ruling class and the esteem afforded her by this position. Her segment reveals both the traditional complacency of the blacks residing on the plantation and the unexpectedness of the elderly black men's rebellion. As she enters the quarters, Myrtle's composure is upset by a vision alien to her conception of the quarters, and she states, "I didn't see any of the people as I drove past the old houses. Just like little bedbugs. . . . Just like frightened little bedbugs now. But when I stopped before Mathu's house, I could see they were not bedbugs after all. They were all there, in the yard, and on the porch. Three of them had shotguns" (*GM*, 15). Myrtle's reference to the "little bedbugs" and her condescending tone betray the paternalism, or in this case "maternalism," that colors her views of black men. Like other white residents of Marshall, she is unable to view the men as men. Her perception of their docility is sharply altered, however, as she witnesses them sitting on the porch, armed. This unexpected image fills Myrtle with incredulity and foreboding, and she articulates her amazement in the statement "I had never seen anything like this in all my life before, and I wasn't too sure I was seeing it now" (*GM*, 15). In voicing the emotional upset engendered by the killing of Beau, Myrtle's narrative contributes a key response to Lou's report and thus accentuates the daring of the old men.

The novel proceeds, detailing a variety of motives, and as a group, the old men's accounts articulate the wrongs committed against an entire race. The section "Robert Louis Stevenson Banks aka Chimley" begins the disclosure of what Beau's killing represents to the black men who seek credit for his death: retribution for loss of family, land, life, and dignity. Chimley recounts the changes in his environment caused by the advent of the Cajuns. His description of being confined to fishing only a small portion of the river indicates that, for him, killing Beau symbolizes reclaiming land and a lifestyle the Cajuns and other whites are increasingly eliminating: "Me and Mat was down there fishing. We goes fishing every Tuesday and every Thursday.

We got just one little spot now. Ain't like it used to be when you had the whole river to fish on. The white people, they done bought up the river now, and you got nowhere to go but that one little spot. . . . Just ain't got nowhere else to go no more" (*GM,* 27). The simplicity in Chimley's observations of shrinking river space masks the severity of the larger social confinement of blacks within a dichotomized environment. The place in which these characters find themselves sequesters them through laws and customs that vigilantly regulate most aspects of their lives. Every decision—from where they may fish, to where they may work, to whom they may love—is decided for them or influenced by larger white society. They are relegated to a world of narrow possibilities and have become accustomed to a life that has told them "you cannot" and "you are not."

The stories of the other men complement Chimley's. One tells of a son who dies when refused treatment at a hospital because he is black; one tells of revenge sought for a sister's rape and death; one details the homecoming of a decorated World War I veteran who must return to the ignominy of segregation; and all contribute to the pageant of historic racial devaluation. As the narratives unfold, it becomes apparent that the men have had no channel for their outrage and have resorted to inaction or self-destructive measures. Now, however, Beau's death gives them a way to express their anger, to redress their losses. Though Beau might not have been the actual agent, for them he is the symbol of the history of oppression they recall in articulating their reasons for wanting revenge.

The men's subjugation is reflected in many ways. In the history of three of the men, for example, the pastoral theme is again employed to illuminate loss of traditions and life. The horse breaker Yank is ironically left broken when the land that supported his living becomes irreversibly altered: "They ain't got no more horses to break no more. The tractors, the cane cutters—and I ain't been nothing ever since. They look at you today and they call you trifling, 'cause they see you sitting there all the time not doing nothing. They can't remember when you used to break all the horses and break all the mules. . . . Well, I remember. I remember. And I know who took it from me, too" (*GM,* 99). A large part of what changes Yank's life is the changing landscape. Cajun technology has taken the land and taken Yank's self-esteem. Though his society demeaned his worth, through horse breaking he was able to hold a position of relative autonomy and stature, but that relative freedom is gone now. For Yank, Beau symbolizes the changing values and traditions that deprived him of a way of living, an identity, and a measure of pride.

Yank's experience is similar to that of two other characters, Tucker and

Johnny Paul. The land, its mutation and mutilation, looms as a large factor in the pair's reasons for wanting Beau dead. As Tucker recalls his brother's dealings with the Cajuns, we see a reincarnation of Raoul Carmier, as a man fights against Cajuns and technology to hold on to the land that formed the basis of his existence. Johnny Paul, in revealing his perception of the Cajun expansion, recalls the spiritual links the Cajuns severed as they consumed land that once was given to blacks. For him, credit for Beau's death becomes a memorial to people and rituals of the past. As he explains his motives to Sheriff Mapes, he portrays the land as a conservator of his ancestry:

You can't see the church with the people, and you can't hear the singing and the praying. You had to be here then to be able to don't see it and don't hear it now. But I was here then, and I don't see it now, and that's why I did it. I did it for them back there under them trees. I did it 'cause that tractor is getting closer and closer to that graveyard, and I was scared if I didn't do it, one day that tractor was go'n . . . plow up them graves, getting rid of all proof that we ever was. (*GM*, 92)

In an idiom resonant with the syntax of his culture, "You had to be here then to be able to don't see it and don't hear it now," Johnny Paul joins other Gaines characters who lament the erasure of African-American history by Cajun tractors and plows.

The potent symbol of his past, represented in the graves of his ancestors, affects the other men in the same fashion it affects Johnny Paul. Their recollections of the wrongs they have endured become catalysts stimulating present action. Their motivation springs from a familiar source in Gaines's canon, a knowledge of and connection to the past. As the men walk through the graveyard on their way to see their plan through to its conclusion, Cherry describes their increasing resolve to take this final stand not only for themselves but for all those who have suffered before them. After giving the history of the cemetery, saying, "That old graveyard had been the burial ground for black folks ever since the time of slavery," Cherry points out the various grave sites that inspire each man, summing up his observations with such comments as "Maybe that's why Jacob was here today" and "Your people will be proud of you" (*GM*, 45–47). The burial plots are reservoirs of ancestry that activate the floodgates of the men's heretofore-unknown strength, creating a current between their history, their present resolve, and the legacy they hope to leave. The unity the men discover in the graveyard transforms them. Old men frail as saplings become an impenetrable forest obscuring the identity of the man they believe to be Beau's killer, Mathu.

Initially, Mathu is the only black man in the novel who has not succumbed to the dehumanization imposed by his society. Throughout his life he has been courageous enough to stand up to the injustices of the plantation order. It is ultimately his example that inspires the others to a new daring. Significantly, Mathu is described as "one of them blue-black Singaleese [Senegalese] niggers" who "[A]lways bragged about not having no white man's blood in his veins" and "looked down on all the rest . . . who had some" (51). The implication of Mathu's description reverses a notion popularized by nineteenth-century writers such as Harriet Beecher Stowe in *Uncle Tom's Cabin* and William Wells Brown in *Clotel*—that the greater amount of white blood a person could claim in his or her heritage, the greater would be his or her desire for freedom.[7] What seems to fuel Mathu's independence and dignity is the purity of his black blood, a purity that enables him to trace his heritage to a proud ancestry in Africa.

Mathu will strike readers as somewhat familiar. He is a male embodiment of Jane Pittman, and a symbol for change because he is a repository of both the black and white pasts. As Candy, a member of the current generation operating Marshall plantation, says to him, "You knew the first. . . . You knew Grandpa Nate. The first Marshall. Remember from the war— the Civil War? . . . Grew up with my grandpa. Raised my daddy. Raised me. I want you to help me with my own child one day. . . . I want you to hold his hand. Tell him about Grandpa. Tell him about the field. Tell him how the river looked before the cabins and the wharves. No one else to tell him about these things but you" (*GM*, 176–77). Because Mathu remembers the plantation's history, he embodies the suffering of the past and the possibility of future change.

Mathu symbolizes the danger assertiveness and dignity pose to the maintenance of black subjugation. The others have secretly admired his demeanor, and now that they assume he has killed Beau and must pay for it, each man decides he must protect the one personification of fearless pride they have. As Mat discusses with his friend Chimley his decision to provide an alibi for Mathu, we see the ultimate influence Mathu has had on his peers:

"You sure now, Chimley?" he said.

"If you go, Mat."

"I have to go, Chimley," he said. "This can be my last chance."

I looked him in the eyes. Lightish-brown eyes. They was saying much more than he said. They was speaking for both of us. . . . His eyes was saying: We wait till now? Now, when we're old men, we get to be brave? (*GM*, 32)

After a lifetime of servitude, the men have found an act to galvanize their dormant courage, and they take a stance they feel they should have taken many years ago. They rally around the man they have long revered, and their strength impresses Lou Dimes into giving the following description: "I suddenly stopped. . . . Like I had run into a brick wall. It was a wall all right, but a wall twenty, thirty feet away from me. Not a wall of brick, stone, or wood, but a wall of old black men with shotguns . . . standing, squatting, sitting. . . . And waiting" (*GM,* 59–60). The wait for the outcome of the day's action is short compared with that experienced by these 70- and 80-year-old males anticipating a day when they could prove themselves men.

It is precisely to prove himself a man that Beau's actual killer returns to confess his crime. Charlie Biggs, known to all as Big Charlie, is characterized by Lou Dimes in terms that conjure the stereotypical image of the black brute: "He was about six seven, he weighed around two hundred and seventy five pounds, he was jet black, with a round cannonball head and his hair cut to the skin; the whites of his eyes were too brown, his lips looked like pieces of liver. His arms bulged inside the sleeves of his denim shirt, and his torso was round as a barrel. . . . He was the quintessence of what you would picture as the super, big buck nigger" (*GM,* 186). Unfortunately, physical stature is the only stature Charlie enjoys, and the small room of Mathu's cabin is the only place where anyone looks up to him. In Marshall Quarters his commanding physical appearance gains him abuse rather than awe. Even though he can "Pull a saw, swing a axe, stretch wire, cut ditch bank, dig postholes, better than any man [he] ever met" (*GM,* 189), in the act that requires the most strength—standing up for his dignity—Charlie's might is negligible.

Charlie tells his story simply and plaintively. At 50, he has been worn down by the degrading social conditions, and his language and observations make him seem more an adolescent than an adult. His recollections of experience are filled with images of impotence and entrapment that illustrate the psychosocial confinement of his world: "I ran, I ran, I ran. . . . But no matter where I went, where I turnt, I was still on Marshall place. If I went toward Pichot . . . something stopped me. If I turnt toward Morgan, something there stopped me too. Something like a wall, a wall I couldn't see, but it stopped me every time" (*GM,* 192). Like the rest of the men, Charlie simply wants recognition of his status as a man. In his world, however, such acceptance is not forthcoming and is in fact replaced with scorn. For the 50 years of his life, he has felt that he must accept dehumanizing treatment and that his only alternatives were to "take it" or to run.

Charlie's initial reaction is consistently to flee abuse, and running has become a lifelong pattern. As he weighs his life, he reflects, "All I ever done ... was run from people. From black, from white; from nigger, from Cajun, both. All my life. Made me do what they wanted me to do, and 'bused me if I did it right, and 'bused me if I did it wrong—all my life. And I took it.... [L]ong as I was Big Charlie, nigger boy, I took it" (*GM*, 188–89). It is actually Mathu, his godfather, who attempts to instill in Charlie the lesson that a man should fight misuse rather than flee, and just as Mathu inspires the other black men in the novel to action, so too does he inspire Charlie to stop running and put an end to his exploitation. Even though it has taken Charlie 50 years to abandon his escapist tendencies, he eventually does reach the point where he is able to assert, "They comes a day when a man must be a man" (*GM*, 189). For Charlie his day arrives when he puts an end to Beau's abuse and kills him.

Like Bigger Thomas after killing Mary Dalton, Charlie experiences a heretofore-unknown self-actualization when he kills Beau. The murder becomes his first act of social impact and serves as a turning point in his life as he rediscovers the pride he thought lost. By killing Beau, he demands the respect he feels is his due, and his new self-esteem and his new conception of himself are evident in the respect he exacts from Sheriff Mapes: "Sheriff, I'm a man.... And just like I call you Sheriff, I think I ought to have a handle, too—like Mister. Mr. Biggs" (*GM*, 187). The title "Mister" confers the social recognition Charlie has lacked, and proves that he is now a man who "did things" rather than a man who runs. The transformation in Charlie's pattern of experience, from running to acting, can be seen in the experience of each of the black men, but the full impact of their bravery is most striking when taken in the context of the narratives the white characters add to the pageant.

As in most of the rural South, in Marshall Quarters forced segregation masks the fact that black and white interact intimately, and the actions of one affect the actions of the other. For a complete vision of the Louisiana world that impels these men to such extreme action, a portrait of the white social psyche is necessary, and with his characteristically diligent attention to voice and point of view Gaines gives his white narrative voices a veracity equal to that of his elderly black men. The result is a realistic and insightful depiction balancing the old men's vision of the universe of their plantation.

Marshall Quarters has attempted to resist change, but as the presence of the Cajuns and the actions of the black men indicate, change cannot be arrested. Candy, Jack, and Beatrice, the last remaining members of the Marshall clan, are symbols of the eroding status quo. The social order that gave their family prominence is gone now, and familial prestige is parceled out with each share of land rented. All the Marshalls are bending under the weight of their family's slaveholding legacy, and each seeks to alleviate the burden in his or her own way—Candy through attempting a sympathetic though at times "maternalistic" relationship with the blacks on the plantation, Jack and Beatrice through remembering and then drinking to forget.

Jack Marshall's bartender, Jacques Thibeaux, like many bartenders is a student of human nature. In watching Jack he perceives the weariness brought on by supporting values that are not his own. Jacques sympathetically delineates the languor that afflicts Jack and represents the declined state of the Marshall lineage:

You know, I sympathize with him. 'Cause you see he never wanted none of this. Never wanted to be responsible for name and land. They dropped it on him, left it on him. That's why he drinks the way he does, and let that niece of his run the place. . . . Get up and drink. Take a little nap, wake up and drink some more. Take another little nap, wake up and come here. Like clockwork. . . . Things just too complicated. I reckon for people like him they have always been complicated— protecting name and land. . . . Feeling guilty about this, guilty about that. (*GM*, 154)

As the legacy of slavery overwhelms Jack, he drinks to induce a stupor that inhibits him from making sense out of the senseless order that fetters him.

Because he prefers dissipation to responsibility, Jack leaves the running of his plantation to Candy. She shares with her uncle a distancing both from the system she is forced to perpetuate and from the way in which that system defines her as a woman. When Beatrice says of Candy, "That gal got spunk" (*GM*, 22), and when Lou Dimes says of her, "*Candy needed me?* I had been knowing Candy for three years, and during all that time I had never known her to need anybody" (*GM*, 58), it is evident that Candy is not cast in the stereotype of the traditional southern belle. "A little, spare woman, not too tall; always wearing pants and shirts, never dresses" (*GM*, 50), Candy defines herself without regard for traditional standards. She is independent, lives by her own values, and forms her own allegiances.

Her strongest allegiance is to Mathu, who has been a surrogate father. He assisted Merle in raising Candy, to ensure her not falling prey to the dissipation that possesses Jack and Beatrice. His contribution to her upbringing afforded her an understanding of black culture to which one of her social position might not be privy, and Lou Dimes explains Candy's second familial association as follows: "After Candy's mother and father died . . . Miss

Merle and Mathu realized that . . . her aunt and uncle . . . were not capable of bringing her up properly, and so took it as their duty to raise her themselves. One to raise her as a lady, the other to make her understand the people who lived on her place. And she had been as close to those two, Miss Merle and Mathu, as she had been to anyone in her life" (*GM*, 129). It is Candy's love for Mathu that prompts her to admit to the killing of Beau and convince the other old men to do the same. Once the old men participate, however, her plan to cover Mathu's suspected guilt evolves into a vehicle of protest demanding social justice long overdue.

Though Candy loves Mathu, she is still white and is still a Marshall. When her plan to protect Mathu begins to take on proportions she did not anticipate, her reaction illustrates the complications caused by conflicting racial allegiance and genuine affection. The men who have adopted her plan reach a point where *they* want to decide what the next course of action must be. Candy is displaced as decision maker and relegated to a position of bystander. In the following interchange among her, Sheriff Mapes, and Clatoo, her good intentions fade as she, upset at being cast aside as the black men now take control of their own destiny, reacts imperiously when the men enter Mathu's cabin to confer on their next tactic:

"Y'all come on inside," Clatoo said to us. "Not you, Candy," he said to her.

"Nobody's talking without me," Candy said. . . .

"This time we have to, Candy," Clatoo said. "Just the men with guns."

"Like hell," Candy said. "This is my place."

"I know that Candy. . . . But we don't want you there this time."

That stopped her. Nobody talked to Candy like that—black or white—and specially not black.

"What the hell did you say? . . . You know who you're talking to? Get the hell off my place. . . ."

"Not till this is cleared up," Clatoo said to her. "I already told the sheriff I don't mind going to jail, or even dying today. And that means I ain't taking no orders either." (*GM*, 173)

When Candy responds to Clatoo's statements with threats of eviction for those who live on her plantation and choose to go against her, the ensuing conversation between her and Sheriff Mapes reveals the "maternalism" of Candy's relationship with blacks:

"Well, well. . . . Listen to the savior now. Do what she wants or you're out in the cold. . . . You want to keep them slaves for the rest of their lives."

"Nobody is a slave here," Candy said. "I'm protecting them like I've always protected them. Like my people have always protected them. Ask them."
   "At least your people let them talk. . . . Now you're trying to take that away
from them." (*GM*, 174)

Candy's desire to "protect" Mathu and the other black men is smattered
with the benevolent racism that allows her to love Mathu and the others but
not recognize their full and complete existence as men. Like the other characters, she is faced with the challenge of leaving a social identity and fully
adopting a personal identity that will allow her to live by values that recognize the sovereignty of the men. Even though she feels stronger ties to
Mathu and the blacks that have coexisted with her family for generations,
social decorum demands that she concede the best land to the Cajuns and
attempt to regulate the decision-making process of the black men. Considering her actions, the question arises, If Mathu were not the man who raised
her as a father, a man who just happened to be black, would Candy resort to
the same extremes to protect him, or might she let the laws of racial injustice
take their own course?
   The divided sentiments Candy feels as she attempts to balance loyalties
across racial lines also affect other characters. Sheriff Mapes, for example, is
just doing his job, and as Joseph "Tufe" Seaberry tells us, likes Mathu:
"Mapes was . . . big, mean, brutal. But Mapes respected a man. Mathu was
a man, and Mapes respected Mathu. . . . They had hunted together. . . .
Fished together. And Mapes had a few drinks with Mathu at Mathu's
house. . . ." (*GM*, 83–84). Similarly, Lou Dimes is only doing his job, reporting what he sees and not passing racial judgments. He can perceive
Mathu's independence and identity even when Candy cannot. He tells her,
"After tonight there's going to be a big change in your life. That old man is
free of you now. When he pulled your hands off his arm . . . he was setting
both of you free. . . . He's an old man, and what little time he's got left he
wants to live it his own way" (*GM*, 185). Even the Cajuns have mixed feelings about how to exact retribution for the death of one of their own. The
complexity of attitudes among the white characters illustrates the ambiguity caused when racial rules regulate genuine human emotion, and the di-
chotomy between social identity and personal identity is most clearly seen in
the divisiveness within the Boutan clan as they attempt to decide how to
avenge Beau's death.
   Fix Boutan, the paternal leader of the clan, is infamous to both blacks
and whites. To those whites who are not Cajuns, he represents the threatening acquisition of a lower class, and to blacks his renown for racially moti-

vated violence makes him a personification of extremism. As he mourns the death of his son Beau, however, he insists his desire to retaliate against the black men waiting with shotguns is motivated not by race but by considerations of family: "This is family. . . . I have no other cause to fight for. I'm too old for causes. . . . A member of the family has been insulted, and family, the family must seek justice" (*GM*, 147). The justice Fix seeks is the justice of "an eye for an eye." Because the accused killer is a black man, he feels justified in taking the law into his own hands and killing any black man for retribution, for all black men are guilty of Beau's murder, by virtue of their color.

Fix is egged on by Luke Will, "one of those big, hulking, beer-belly rednecks" (*GM*, 141). Luke is an anachronism, needing black blood to supply a sense of power and social status that in reality he lacks. His craving for revenge arises not out of his love for Beau but out of his hatred of blacks and resentment of his own relative social impotence as a Cajun. His description of his and Beau's friendship—"I was closer than a friend. . . . I was a good friend. We had a beer last night" (136)—lacks the passion of his rally to arms: "When niggers start shooting down white men in broad daylight, the trouble was started. . . . Somebody got to [settle] it 'fore it gets out of hand. . . . Next thing you know, they'll be raping the women" (149). Luke's statements reveal a mind capable only of simplistic reasoning, equating friendship with the sharing of a beer, and the slaughter of blacks with the archaic notion of preserving white feminine purity.

The values of Fix and Luke are no longer appropriate in the Marshall Quarters of the 1970s, and the relationship between Gil Boutan, Fix's youngest son, and his college teammate, Calvin Harrison, reflects change in racial attitudes. Known as "Salt" and "Pepper," Gil and Cal together are the reason for the success of Louisiana State University's football team: "Both were good powerful runners, and excellent blockers. Gil blocked for Cal on sweeps around end, and Cal returned the favor when Gil went up the middle. . . . On the gridiron they depended on each other the way one hand must depend on the other swinging a baseball bat" (*GM*, 112–15). The racial unity they symbolize has caught the attention of "the black and white communities in Baton Rouge" and "the rest of the country" (*GM*, 112). It is precisely because of this unity that Gil can no longer live by his father's dictates.

When he returns home, Gil pleads with his father not to become a vigilante. He has come to cherish his position in the public eye as an all-American and wants no racial vendetta to besmirch it. An astute young man, he is very aware of the social stratifications of his world. His insights again call William Faulkner to mind, as the class divisions among southern whites permeate his relationship with the Marshalls. Gil is aware that Candy, as a descendant of the traditional white ruling class, looks down on his people as "a breed below." He is also aware of the motivations behind the actions of Luke Will, and he seeks to distance himself and his family from the likes of Will, telling his father, "Those days . . . when you just take the law in your own hands . . . are gone. These are the '70s, soon to be the '80s. Not the '20s, the '30s, or the '40s. . . . Luke Will and his gang are a dying breed. They need a cause like this to pump blood back into their dying bodies. . . . But I would like people to know we're not what they think we are. They all expect us to ride tonight. . . . I say let them wait" (*GM*, 143). By showing his father he must define himself by new values, Gil persuades him to live by the law, and symbolically takes over as head of the Boutan family, moving it into a new era.

The dependency shared by Gil and Cal on the football field is one that Gaines, as a literary observer, sees shared by blacks and whites of the South. The history and legacy of slavery and the advent of sharecropping have left the two races in such close quarters that neither can define their existence without the inclusion of the other. The inequities of white supremacy have affected all the characters of Marshall Quarters, black and white, in very real and human terms, becoming for blacks a burden of oppression and for whites a burden of culpability. A white schoolteacher, taking a drink in the same bar as Luke Will, pleads with him not to carry out his racial vendetta, "[F]or the sake of the South," knowing that such a vendetta only makes ponderous the already-weighty burdens of subjugation and guilt.

The close intertwining of blacks and whites in this Louisiana parish and the senseless violence that has existed between them make the confrontation with which Gaines closes the novel bizarre and at points humorous. Three key references made in the novel—to Stephen Crane's *Red Badge of Courage,* to the television series "The Twilight Zone," and to the painter Jan Brueghel—now add fullness to the meaning of the final scenes of the work.

It is Thomas Vincent Sullivan, a.k.a. Sully or T.V., who comments upon the sharp contrast between the men and their environment and makes reference to both "The Twilight Zone" and possibly Jan Brueghel:

[W]e were coming up to the junction that said St. Charles River, . . . It was a good straight road for about four miles, with the sugarcane fields on either side. Much of the cane had been cut, and far across the field on the right side of the road was that dark line of trees which was the beginning of the swamps. . . . [W]e made the turn that took us along the St. Charles River. The river was grayish blue, and very calm. . . .

Just as we turned into Marshall Quarters, I noticed a patrolman's car parked beside the road. . . . There in the yard on the porch were all these old men with shotguns. . . . Every last one of them was looking back at us. It was like looking into the *Twilight Zone*. . . . You would be driving through this little out-of-the-way-town, and suddenly you would come upon a scene that you knew shouldn't be there—it was something like that. Something like looking at a Brueghel painting. One of these real, weird, weird Brueghels. (*GM,* 116–18)

The reference to Jan Brueghel connects Gaines's use of the pastoral to the murder and the bizarre events it will engender. It is fairly typical of Brueghel's style to depict war scenes in a deceptively pastoral manner. Taking one of his better-known paintings, *The Battle of Issus* (1602), as an example, images of war are meshed into images of the natural landscape. Against an Edenic, tranquil background of trees and sky, suffused with what might be the mist of dew is the scene of a bloody battle. The frontmost section of the painting is heavily peopled with those fighting and their bloodied casualties, but as the viewer's eye travels to the backdrop of the painting, warriors in helmets are gently brushed into boughs, and men with weapons become trees and branches. The effect is to make the viewer return to the foreground of the painting to reconcile a picture in which the mist of nature is transformed into a battle and a battle is transformed into a misty pastoral. The technique of this painting is transformed into a literary medium as Gaines constantly foregrounds images of the men's insurrectionist stance against the quiet of the cane fields, the swamp, and the St. Charles River.

In the dark, with the bushes surrounding Mathu's house as their backdrop, the old black men wage a war they have been yearning to fight. The scene is surreal, and as Sully points out, characteristic of "The Twilight Zone." A new dimension of existence has been entered as old men throw off the traditional definitions assigned them and face the subjugators they have appeased for so many years. They engage in a shooting battle against the opponents they have been unable to fight, and even if they miss their mark, some hitting the ceiling of Mathu's house, they are satisfied, knowing they have taken a shot at liberty. At long last they taste self-esteem, and for the first time they realize that "Life's so sweet when you know you ain't no more coward" (*GM,* 208). With each volley the black men release a cry of freedom, each giving it a phraseology of his own. Some yell, some "hoot," and Yank performs a "ya-hoo," reminiscent of a rodeo cowboy. Their new bearing seems otherworldly to the opposing whites, who are left wondering, "[W]hat them niggers been drinking to make them all so brave?" (*GM*, 204).

The bizarre events continue to the courtroom scene, in which Gaines deftly shows, through humor, the senselessness of racial hatred and the pride of men who have discovered their dignity. As the final segment opens, the courtroom is peopled with representatives of the racial polarization that leads to the events of the novel: "The Klans and the Nazi Party were there to lend moral support to Luke Will's friends. The NAACP was there, some black militants were there" (*GM*, 212). Lou Dimes is appropriately the narrator of this final portion, and as a reporter he gives the following account of the remaining defendants: "You've never seen a sadder bunch of killers in all your life—on either side. Everybody had something wrong with him— scratches, bruises, cuts, gashes. They had cut themselves on barbed wire, tin cans, broken bottles—you name it. Some had sprained their ankles jumping over ditches; others had sprained their wrists falling down on the ground. And some had just run into each other. Everybody was either limping, his arm in a sling, or there was a bandage around his head or some other part of his body" (*GM*, 211). Lou's description of the scene before him is laced with both humor and pathos. The men he describes are warriors of an absurd war, and their appearance leaves one wondering why these men had to fight in the first place. The irony that emerges here echoes the irony of Stephen Crane's *The Red Badge of Courage*, in which the glory of war is called into question by its brutal actuality.

Each description in the courtroom scene becomes increasingly comedic and appears to lessen the profoundness of the men's confrontation, leading Lou to comment, "[E]veryone in the courtroom started laughing. . . . The people passing by out on the street must have thought we were showing a Charlie Chaplin movie" (*GM*, 213). Humor is capped with hyperbole, as each man, "knowing he was in the public eye, would go just a little over-board describing what had happened" (*GM*, 212). At long last the men have an opportunity to assert themselves, their personalities, and relish their moment in the spotlight. When Lou reports that the "news people . . . took the whole thing as something astonishing but not serious" (*GM*, 212), the import of the men's act teeters on the brink of being lost. But when Lou Dimes observes, "No one else laughed nearly as much as the news people did" (*GM*, 212), we are reminded that the media are outsiders, people not steeped in the history of Marshall plantation, and therefore people unable to understand the larger implications of the courtroom drama. The indige-nous populace of Marshall Quarters know that what has brought them to court is an act of revolution, one in which a group of black men demanded the respect that is their due, and in so doing stood the conventions of their social system on end. The full significance of their act is most lucidly revealed in the last paragraph of the novel.

As Lou and Candy stand on the court steps at the close of the proceedings, he details a significant interaction between Candy and Mathu: "Candy and I went out of the courtroom and stood out on the steps and watched the people leave. She asked Mathu if he wanted her to take him back home. He told her no; he told her Clatoo was there in the truck, and he would go back with Clatoo and the rest of the people. . . . Candy waved goodbye to them. I felt her other hand against me, searching for my hand; then I felt her squeezing my fingers" (*GM*, 214). Just as Mathu goes home with "the rest of the people," in effect the rest of *his* people, so too must Candy return to her people and her world, as represented in Lou's presence and her squeezing his hand. The "maternalistic" bond that has joined her and Mathu is broken, for the new dignity that Mathu and his community have seized necessitates the creation of a new and independent existence.

The men at the close of the novel, in their best clothes, proudly retelling the act that has made them men again, are vastly different from the stooped, overburdened men who begin the novel. Their collective confession has purged them of the impotent rage they have nurtured against the plantation system, but more importantly it has purged them of the self-loathing they have harbored for the majority of their lives. Through the telling of their stories, through the emotional truth of their symbolic if not actual killing of Beau Boutan, they confront their past and restructure their present and future.

The revolution enacted by these men is a quiet one, indicative of Gaines's attitude that the best change is slow and quiet change. Like Jane Pittman, these men have used the weapons that stem from their own culture—the memory of history, their family and friends, the recent memory of their abuse—to finally mount an attack they have previously been too fearful to mount. Their strength is an evolving strength that will engender a legacy of change that is gradual yet lasting.

Chapter Eight
Finding the Voice to Tell the Story

In his preface to *God's Trombones* James Weldon Johnson outlines a possible poetics for the creation of black poetry: "The Negro poet in the United States, for poetry which he wishes to give a distinctly racial tone and color, needs now an instrument of greater range than dialect; . . . he needs to find a form that will express the racial spirit by symbols from within rather than by symbols from without."[1] We can extend Johnson's observation to encompass prose literature, for he articulates a problem faced by many African-American writers: finding stylistic forms appropriate for the expression of black experience.

It is certainly true that every writer grapples with questions of form, whether it is a regionalist such as Mark Twain, who through Huck Finn, to name one character, embodied a portion of the American spirit not previously found in literature, or a modernist such as Gertrude Stein, who experimented with language and narrative structure in an attempt to create literature that captured the disaffected spirit of American expatriates of the post–World War I epoch. For the black author in the United States, however, questions of form are complicated by considerations of race. Whether a writer elects to create a text specifically addressing race, or not, to use the language, symbols, and traditions of the black race, or not, the specter of the author's ethnicity is often present, if not in the content of the text then in its evaluation.

Whether there is or should be a specifically black aesthetic has been hotly debated since the inception of African-American literature. For some writers a racial criterion poses an unfair burden, but for others racial experience readily suggests aesthetic form. Ernest Gaines falls into the latter group of writers. Indeed he is so comfortable in his identity as "a black writer" that his canon peaceably reconciles complexities that have dogged black literature since its inception.

Born of the slave narratives, African-American literature has continually addressed the injustices felt by black Americans as they were first slaves, then strangers in their own house. When such authors as Frederick Douglass, Harriet Wilson, and William Wells Brown created early African-American works, their primary goals were the revelation of slavery's abuses and its subsequent abolition. Thematically, the choice for writers of the slave narratives and literature loosely based on the narrative, such as Brown's *Clotel* or Harriet Wilson's *Our Nig,*[2] was a clear one: how best to evoke the horrors of slavery and indentured servitude to implicate the reader and spur him or her to demand progressive change. To that end, accounts of physical brutality in the form of habitual and arbitrary beatings, of rape and sexual exploitation, of the rending of husband from wife and parent from child, and of the routine dehumanization contrived to eradicate any trace of personal identity compose the core of these writings aimed at salvaging moral conscience.

The stylistic choice offered these writers was no less clear, where a choice even existed. Slaves were forbidden by law to read or write, and punishment could be arbitrarily severe at the slaveholder's discretion. Many of the narratives that do exist were recounted by amanuenses, most of whom were white abolitionists. While sympathetic to the cause and content of the narratives, the majority of these abolitionists acted as editors, molding the accounts to a particular model and perhaps deleting many of the cadences that might have served as the foundation for an African-American aesthetic, replacing them with nineteenth-century literary conventions.[3] Those African-American writers who did pen their own narratives sought to prove their cognitive capability and their worthiness of equal social and political status through an imitation of the prevailing literary aesthetic. If we can write as you, they reasoned, surely we are able to think as you, and so should we not be treated as you? Many expressed this plea in the form of poetic soliloquies, elaborate textual allusions, and Elizabethan phrasing. While it is the most eloquent of the slave narratives, even *The Narrative of Frederick Douglass* is highly derivative as it aims to decry slavery and demand equality.

What did endure of a possible African-American aesthetic abided in the spirituals and the oral tales of the slaves. Ironically, but indicative of a larger, persistent pattern of appropriation, it would first be authors whose color freed them from laboring under the burden of proving themselves equal who would hear and respond to the folk repository of black America and place it in their literature. While the nineteenth-century white literary establishment denounced the vulgarity of black dialect, the reading public clamored for the works of Thomas Nelson Page and Joel Chandler Harris precisely because of the nostalgic vision of race relations personified through

docile black characters who spoke in dialect and subtly reinforced a suprem-
acist ideology.[4]

The precedent of Page's and Harris's use of black materials would become burdensome to black writers in the early twentieth century. Such writers as Paul Laurence Dunbar and Charles Chesnutt, who would employ
traditions and forms deriving from African-American culture, often felt coercion rather than desire to do so. Some of Dunbar's critics preferred the
"quaintness" of his dialect poems to the intensity of those composed in standard English, and as an artist Dunbar suffered for it. He voiced his torment
in his plaintive poem "The Poet." Charles Chesnutt suffered similarly from
the demand of a white reading public that craved the novelty of black stere-
otypes. Though in *The Conjure Woman* he used the frame story to distance
himself safely from the artistic crudeness attributed to black dialect, and
while he ardently rendered the tragedies of black enslavement and dehumanization, the majority of his white readers saw only the resemblance of
his narrator, Julius McAdoo, to Harris's Uncle Remus and equated his poli-
ticized use of dialect with Harris's romantic use of the form to minimize the
adversity of black life.

Beginning in the 1920s, with the advent of the Harlem Renaissance,
black writers sought to free themselves from the constraints felt by writers
like Chesnutt and Dunbar. But while most agreed with the aims of the
Harlem Renaissance and realized they were the ones who should create and
define a genuine black aesthetic, the avenue to artistic liberation was unclear. Exploring African, Caribbean, and rural southern cultures, writers un-
earthed aesthetic forms they felt might be suitable for articulating black
experience, and the result was a confluence of African-American forms in
literature. Not all writers were at ease with forms indigenous to black culture, however. While some, such as Zora Neale Hurston, were comfortable
in meshing dialect and vernacular constructs of the South into literary prose,
others, such as James Weldon Johnson, still feeling the presence of a white
reading public, shunned their overt incorporation. Yet elements from
African-American culture—the black preacher, jazz, and the blues, for
example—gave many black writers of the Harlem Renaissance, such as
Langston Hughes, stylistic avenues to explore as they mapped the shape of
their texts.

The Harlem Renaissance sparked a restatement of African-American
calls for political and social equality, and a similar restatement would occur
again in the 1960s and 1970s. A second black renaissance would also be
evident in literature and would again present black writers with many of the
stylistic dilemmas faced by their predecessors. The question of a black writ-

er's role and audience was heatedly debated in the 1960s, and a 1968 *Negro Digest* poll elicited a wide range of opinions. Alice Walker and Etheridge Knight are two examples. In her response to the journal's questionnaire, Walker wrote the following about black writers in America and their literature:

To write solely for a black audience is limiting and presumes too much: that they will appreciate your efforts; that they will try to understand you; that they will care enough about your work to buy your books; and that white people could never get anything (be made better, one might say) from what one writes. . . .

I think it is only important that we write from within ourselves and that we direct our efforts outward. Period. I would have liked for Victor Hugo to like my stories quite as much as I admire his.[5]

Etheridge Knight responded in a different manner:

The white aesthetic would tell the Black Artist that *all* men have the same problems, that all try to find their dignity and identity, that we are all brothers and blah blah blah. . . .

Unless the Black Artist establishes a "black aesthetic" he will have no future at all. To accept the white aesthetic is to accept and validate a society that will not allow him to live. The Black Artist must create new forms and new values, sing new songs (or purify old ones); and along with other Black Authorities, he must create a new history, new symbols, myths and legends (and purify the old ones by fire). And, the Black Artist, in creating his own aesthetic, must be accountable for it only to the black people. ("LL," 38)

Whatever the individual response, the question of a black aesthetic affected almost every black writer. In the midst of this debate, however, a collected Ernest Gaines would continue writing of his southern Louisiana world in his unique manner.

Considering the many literary movements contemporaneous to his career as a writer, it is extraordinary that Gaines has remained so dedicated to his personal vision of what a black writer should be and do. Though he lived and wrote in San Francisco during the time of that city's literary renaissance, he stands independent of the concerns expressed by Allen Ginsberg and Jack Kerouac. Though he writes during the change and upheaval of the 1960s and 1970s, he does not construct a literature of obvious racial or political protest. Central to his vision is "People. People. People" ("LL," 27). In the same *Negro Digest* poll, Gaines outlines his vision of aesthetics and audience, a vision still evident even in his most recent fiction: "I've always said that a man, black writer or not, should do what he can do best. . . . The artist is the only free man left. He owes nobody nothing—not even himself. He should write what he wants, when he wants, and to whomever he wants. If he is true, he will use that material which is closest to him. Those people who have experienced much of what he (the artist) has will see themselves in his work. If they don't then no amount of preaching by the artist will do any good" ("LL," 27).

As a black writer, Gaines has been criticized for his seeming political neutrality, but close readings of his work reveal that he is impassioned by the cause of political and social equality. All his characters seek justice and recognition but do so on personal terms. The lessons that James's mother in "The Sky Is Gray" strives so hard to teach him are lessons in maintaining dignity as a young black man despite a segregated society that attempts to strip him of self-esteem. Proctor Lewis in "Three Men" takes a stance that will lead to his incarceration precisely because he wants his society to deem black life worthy. Marcus Payne in *Of Love and Dust,* Jane Pittman in *The Autobiography,* and the elderly men in *A Gathering of Old Men* all mount their own personally fashioned protests against the social treatment deeded them.

Gaines's fiction is filled with political nuances, and historic movements from Reconstruction to the civil rights movement are evident in many of his texts. In *The Autobiography of Miss Jane Pittman,* Jimmy Aaron in the 1960s continues the battle for civil rights that Ned Douglass began during the period of Reconstruction. Aunt Fe, the pillar of her community in "Just like a Tree," faces uprooting because one of her charges deems civil rights vital to the existence of their community. The creation of Phillip Martin in *In My Father's House* is informed by Martin Luther King, and the naming of Phillip's son conjures associations to Malcolm X. Gaines is clearly aware of and concerned with political events, but he is more concerned with the universal and constant human passions that give rise to these events within the society he has created. The desperation that causes Copper Laurent in "Bloodline" to create a fictitious army to fight for his and others' birthrights stems from an anger directed at an unfair society, the same anger that propels Marcus into miscegenation. For Gaines, society and politics are not abstracts; they are part of the human condition and are rendered in human terms within his literature.

It is precisely politics that restricts all Gaines's characters. The determining factors of race and social class confine all. His white plantation owners know they are bound to upholding a decaying system that entraps them as it does the blacks caught within it, yet they refuse to transgress the laws of its imposed order. Though Frank Laurent in "Bloodline" and Jack Marshall

in *A Gathering of Old Men* almost break under the weight of their social leg-
acies, they still feel compelled by their race and lineage to maintain them.
Gaines's black characters are even more confined, and those who do com-
mit the hubris of demanding a change to the order flee, suffer, or die.
Marcus and Louise in *Of Love and Dust* are its actual victims, and Jackson
Bradley in *Catherine Carmier* is made rootless by its forces.

A regionalist writer in the tradition of Zora Neale Hurston and William
Faulkner, Gaines addresses the social implications of race and class in terms
stemming from the rural Louisiana world he depicts in his works. More important than theoretical sociopolitical issues are characters' internal desires
and passions and how they position themselves in relation to their immediate society and environment. The larger issues of cultural displacement, the
friction between a past and a future, and the quest for manhood are rendered respectively in the very southern images of black displacement by Cajuns, the decay of plantation families, and young, mature, and old males
learning how to be men within a segregated society. In her review of *Miss
Jane*, Alice Walker describes how Gaines deftly balances his art and his politics by grounding his writing in southern experience and creating a universal
literature:

Because politics are strung throughout this rich and very big novel, it will no doubt
be said that Gaines's book is about politics. But he is too skilled a writer to be stuck
in so sordid, so small a category. . . . There is nothing in Gaines that is not open to
love or interpretation. He also claims and revels in the rich heritage of Southern
black people and their customs; the community he feels with them is unmistakable
and goes deeper even than pride. . . . Gaines is mellow with historical reflection,
supple with wit, relaxed and expansive because he does not equate his people with
failure.[6]

Walker correctly captures Gaines's focus on the personal manifestations of
heroism in his southern characters. Their most remarkable trait is their endurance, their ability to begin again. Though he has lost his stature in his
community and his first son, Phillip Martin begins again to rediscover his
integrity; though she is 110 years old, Jane Pittman undertakes a new journey in Bayonne to gain access to the courthouse to which she has been denied entry; though they must leave the plantations they call home, both
Jackson Bradley and Jim Kelly set out to find new lives for themselves.
Gaines's characters reflect the fluidity of life, and the manner in which he
tells their stories readily suggests a form that, for Gaines, resolves the debate
over a black aesthetic.

Coming from a long line of storytellers or "liars," and wanting to incorporate a rural southern view of the world of his fiction, Gaines draws upon a rich cultural reservoir of folk materials, particularly those of the South: spirituals give his themes a timelessness within black history; the rhetoric of the black church and folk sermons gives his prose unique rhythm; the recollections of former slaves suggest a form through which he can personalize testaments to the moral corruption caused by adamant race and caste attitudes; African-derived systems of belief, such as hoodoo, give him images and vehicles for fictional development; and the oral tradition gives him the structure to house all these elements of black culture. He brings the black folk past to life and empowers the written word by rooting it in the oral traditions of his native Louisiana. In his style, his emphasis on the telling of a story and his flawless ear for the language of his South are evident. Whether it be the chronicling of a woman's journey from slavery to freedom or the complex interaction of the cultural groups of Louisiana—the whites, blacks, Cajuns, and Creoles—Gaines renders experience as if it is being passed on from one storyteller to the next. He continues what many began before him on his Aunt Augusteen's porch: the interpretation and continuance of existence. As such, his works often seem to be segments of an ongoing saga.

In an unusual sense, Gaines is grounded in the modernist tradition as he mutates the conventions of earlier prose literature, not to embody the new but to embrace the old. His narrative structure represents a remarkably political act of a modernist writer. He has taken a form traditionally inhospitable to oral cultures, the written word, and transformed it, making it responsive to the needs of a rich oral reservoir. The larger society he depicts in his fiction is not only one in which white dominates black; it is also one in which literacy dominates orality. By focusing his fiction on the smaller community within this society, the quarters, Gaines effects a reorganization of the written-oral hierarchy and defines a possible "black aesthetic" using the "liars" of his community, the hoodoo of Louisiana, the history of slavery, and the quest for human dignity.

Gaines has reconstructed his Pointe Coupée experience and given it larger meaning for a diverse audience. His images, metaphors, and characters create writing so vivid it transcends African-American experience and voices the concerns of humanity. He has meshed symbols from within with symbols from without and created a literature at once personal and universal.

Notes and References

Chapter One

1. For further information on *griots* and the etymology of the term, see Ruth Finnegan, *Oral Literature in Africa* (London: Oxford University Press–Clarendon, 1970).

2. In an interview Gaines describes the passing of the Pointe Coupée that appears in his literature: "I came from a plantation. I wish someday we could go down there. The old houses are being torn down; the cemetery is still there. All the things are being torn down. There are one or two houses still there though. They are just as they were. . . . [A]n old man who lives there now says they were built during slavery. So these things are over a hundred years old, and they're there still. I like to catch the feeling of that place" (Forest Ingram and Barbara Steinberg, "On the Verge: An Interview with Ernest Gaines," *New Orleans Review* 3, no. 4 [1972]: 339; hereafter cited in text).

3. "Miss Jane and I," special issue of *Callaloo* 1, no. 3 (May 1978): 25; hereafter cited in text as "MJ and I."

4. In "Miss Jane and I," Gaines elaborates on these and other literary influences that aided in the creation of his fiction (31).

5. Sara Blackburn, review of *Of Love and Dust, Bergen [New Jersey] Record,* 24 April 1977, B4.

6. In "Miss Jane and I," Gaines discusses his relationship to his most famous character (36–37).

7. Charles H. Rowell, "'This Louisiana Thing That Drives Me': An Interview with Ernest J. Gaines," *Callaloo* 1, no. 3 (May 1978): 40; hereafter cited in text.

8. Paul Desruisseaux, "Ernest Gaines: A Conversation," *New York Times Book Review,* 11 June 1978, 45; hereafter cited in text.

9. In his article "Bayonne or the Yoknapatawpha of Ernest Gaines," Michel Fabre delineates the symbolic importance of the Cajuns to Gaines's fictional world: "Descendants of unhappy Acadians chased out of Canada and sold by Napoleon, the Cajuns became ruthless poor whites who got the best pieces of land. They formed a united front and threatened any new property owners" (*Callaloo* 1, no. 3 [May 1978]: 112–13; hereafter cited in text). For further history and information on the Cajuns of this part of Louisiana, see Carl Brasseaux, *The Founding of New Acadia: The Beginnings of Acadian Life in Louisiana 1765–1803* (Baton Rouge: Louisiana State University Press, 1987). For a more current anthropological study of Cajun life, see Marjorie Esman, *Henderson, Louisiana: Cultural Adaptation in a Cajun Community* (New York: Holt Rinehart & Winston, 1985). Cajun impact on

Gaines's real and fictitious worlds will be treated more thoroughly in the chapter discussing *Catherine Carmier.*

10. Fred Beauford, "A Conversation with Ernest Gaines," *Black Creation* 4 (Fall 1972): 16–17; hereafter cited in text.

11. *Callaloo* 1, no. 3 (May 1978): 53–67.

12. John Henry and Singalee Black Harriet are popular figures in African-American folklore. John Henry has represented human triumph over dehumanization; Singalee Black Harriet, slaves who "escaped" bondage through insanity. For more information on both, see Alan Dundes, ed., *Mother Wit from the Laughing Barrel: Readings in the Interpretation of Afro-American Folklore* (Englewood Cliffs, N.J.: Prentice Hall, 1973), and Zora Neale Hurston, *Mules and Men* (Bloomington: Indiana University Press, 1963).

Chapter Two

1. Robert Gemmet and Philip Gerber, "An Interview: Ernest J. Gaines." *New Orleans Review* 1 (Summer 1969): 334; hereafter cited in text.

2. *Bloodline* (New York: W. W. Norton, 1976), 3; hereafter cited in text as *BL.*

3. Of the meaning of the car within his story Gaines states, "[I]n 'A Long Day in November,' the first story in *Bloodline* . . . I made a comedy that the father gets involved in mechanical things. Or gets involved in anything else but the education of the son. The true education of the son. But it means much more than that. It was a symbol. It symbolizes this crazy mechanized world" (Beauford, 18). In "The Pain and the Beauty: The South, the Black Writer, and the Conventions of the Picaresque," J. Lee Greene elaborates on the tension of nature and technology found in the works of southern black writers. His comments give additional insight helpful in understanding Gaines's use of nature and technology in his treatment of Eddie and subsequent characters who are forced to confront the effects of modernization: "While his soul is nourished by his natural environment, the body of the southern black character is victimized by 'the Man,' by the white South that tempts him with its increasing materialistic assets. Tempted and then seduced by the tantalizing rewards of the new society's materialism and technology, the black character is primed for the destruction of his body and soul when he tries to gain access to the fruits of this society through its social, political, and economic institutions" (Louis D. Rubin, Jr., ed., *The American South: Portrait of a Culture* [Baton Rouge: Louisiana State University Press, 1980], 265).

4. Albert J. Raboteau, *Slave Religion: "The Invisible Institution" in the Antebellum South* (New York: Oxford University Press, 1978), ix; hereafter cited in text.

5. W. E. B. Du Bois, *The Souls of Black Folk* (New York: Penguin, 1989), 155. For information on the role of the black preacher and the use of religion during and after slavery, see Eugene D. Genovese, *Roll Jordan Roll* (New York:

Pantheon/Random, 1974), and John Brown Childs, *The Political Black Minister* (Boston: G. K. Hall, 1980).

6. The terms *hoodoo, rootwork,* and *conjure* are often used interchangeably. Of the distinction between voodoo and hoodoo Raboteau gives the following history: "Hoodoo . . . was a system of magic, divination, and herbalism widespread among the slaves. Since New Orleans was looked upon as the prestigious center of conjuring, the term 'voodoo' was extended to conjuring and conjurers throughout the United States regardless of the term's original reference to African-Haitian cults. Hoodoo became the name for a whole area of folklore, the realm of signs, powers, and conjuring" (80).

7. Melville J. Herskovits's *The Myth of the Negro Past* (Boston: Beacon Press, 1958) gives a thorough and insightful investigation of Africanisms that persist in African-American religion (153–54, 207–60). For further information on the function of conjure and hoodoo men and women, see Zora Neale Hurston's *Mules and Men* (Bloomington: Indiana University Press, 1978). For a record of how former slaves felt about the powers of conjure and hoodoo, see B. A. Botkin, ed., *Lay My Burden Down: A Folk History of Slavery* (Chicago: University of Chicago Press, 1945), 29–38. For a fictional treatment of conjure, see Charles Chesnutt, *The Conjure Woman* (Ann Arbor: University of Michigan Press, 1972).

8. Gaines admits to an autobiographical influence in creating James's experience. He states, "In each story I've myself gone through much of the same experience as these kids have. . . . I had a toothache when I was a child at that age, and I had to ride the bus, just as he rides. At that time, on a bus in the South, you had a little sign hanging over the aisle and it said 'White' on one side and it said 'Colored' on the other side, and you had to sit behind that little sign. . . . I also went to a Catholic school in this little town, which I call Bayonne in the story. I also could not eat uptown. There was no place for me to eat; whether it was cold or sleet or rain. . . . There was no place to warm a child eight years old. To do it, a mother had to take him back of town, which was about a mile, 3/4 of a mile, something like that, and there was no transportation unless someone picked you up when they saw you walking by. . . . I also knew about the dentist's waiting room. . . . Of course, there were all black people in here: the whites were sitting someplace else" (Gemmett and Gerber, 334–35).

9. The preacher's inability to respond verbally can be viewed as an indication of his impotency as an African-American leader. If one of the hallmarks of leadership within the black religious tradition is the ability to manipulate the verbal medium, and the black preacher is a potent symbol of oral power, then this preacher's muteness might signify both frustration with and alienation from the tradition that historically has given him power.

10. The technique of masking refers to a mode of behavior that allows black Americans to survive while maintaining some element of dignity within a hostile racial situation. Elaborating on the term, J. Lee Greene states, "The . . . ability to survive by . . . wits . . . is shared by southern black characters in life and in litera-

ture. The Black American has endured the brutalities of a slave existence, the oppressive practices of Jim Crow, the lynching mania that spread over the South from the end of the Civil War until the end of the third decade of this century, and other threats to his survival. The New World African learned to adapt to his New World conditions, taught his descendants how to survive under these conditions, and never accepted these conditions as definitive of his proper station in American life. Out of the folk culture come tales of this adaptation. . . . From these tales . . . comes what I term the mask device. The device is apparent in several accounts of slave life and slave escapes. To be sure, the various disguises slaves used to deceive their masters and whites in general are indicative of the strategy blacks have used for centuries to survive in America (281–82).

11. Gaines gives background on the experience that inspired the story: "[A] friend of mine and I were talking, and during our conversation he told me that another friend of ours had been killed by another black man in Baton Rouge, and that the person who had killed him was sent to prison for only a short time and then released. . . . Then I recalled hearing about two other incidents in which blacks had murdered blacks. In Case One, when a white lawyer offered his services for a small fee, the prisoner told him that he would rather go to the pen and pay for his crime. But in Case Two the prisoner left with his white employer. Remembering the first incident, I wrote the long story, 'Three Men,' which was published in my *Bloodline* collection of stories" ("MJ and I," 33).

12. Frederick Douglass, *The Narrative of Frederick Douglass, an American Slave* (New York: Penguin, 1982), 89–90.

13. There are many works of literature in which the tragic mulatto figure is used as a symbol of the complications of cross-racial interaction. Among African-American authors, classic texts include William Wells Brown's *Clotel; or, The President's Daughter* (New York: Collier, Macmillan 1970); Charles W. Chesnutt's *The Wife of His Youth and Other Stories* (Ann Arbor: University of Michigan Press, 1972) and *The Marrow of Tradition* (Ann Arbor: University of Michigan Press, 1970); and James Weldon Johnson's *Autobiography of an Ex-Colored Man* (New York: Hill & Wang, 1960). Among white American authors, such books include Harriet Beecher Stowe's *Uncle Tom's Cabin* (New York: Penguin, 1981) and Mark Twain's *Pudd'nhead Wilson* (New York: Penguin, 1977).

14. In this work, which is as much slave narrative as it is novel, the president to whom Brown refers is Thomas Jefferson. Throughout history a rumor has persisted that Jefferson fathered five children by his slave mistress, Sally Hemings, the half-sister of his wife, Martha Jefferson. In her biography of Jefferson, Fawn M. Brodie gives the following account of the rumor: "The story of the slave mistress was first published in detail by scandalmonger and libeler of presidents James Thomson Callender in the *Richmond Recorder* in 1802–3. Callender, who had learned from neighbors of Jefferson the gossip that he had fathered five children by Sally Hemings, wrote of her in some detail, and stated that the features of the oldest, Tom, 'are said to bear a striking although sable resemblance to those of the

president himself'" (*Thomas Jefferson: An Intimate History* [New York: W. W. Norton, 1974], 31). She also states that "[B]eyond . . . generalized protests at Callender's slander, Jefferson would . . . make no specific denials about Sally Hemings in public or private" (361). Though historians continue to debate the existence of Jefferson's black children, no conclusive documentation that might shed light on the story's verity or falsity has been discovered. According to Brodie, "The one record that might illuminate this, the letter-index volume recording Jefferson's incoming and outgoing letters for this critical year of 1788, has disappeared. It is the only volume missing in the whole forty-three-year epistolary record" (234). In his novel Brown crafts a fictitious character, Clotel, based on Jefferson's supposed daughter and uses Jefferson's relationship with Hemings to address the hypocrisy of a society whose preeminent defender of democratic principles is also a slaveholder and the father of illegitimate black children. In fashioning Clotel, Brown creates one of the earliest fictional treatments of miscegenation in African-American literature, and describes the plight of the tragic mulatto in the following terms: "[O]ne so white seldom ever receives fair treatment at the hands of his fellow slaves; and the whites usually regard such slaves as persons who, if not often flogged, and otherwise ill treated, to remind them of their condition, would soon 'forget' that they were slaves, and 'think themselves as good as white folks'" (*Clotel*, 181).

15. Alvin Aubert, "Ernest Gaines's Truly Tragic Mulatto," *Callaloo* 1, no. 3 (May 1978): 69.

16. John F. Callahan, "Hearing Is Believing: The Landscape of Voice in Ernest Gaines's *Bloodline*," *Callaloo* 7, no. 1 (Winter 1984): 107.

17. When asked in an interview whether Faulkner was an influence in the story's structure, Gaines replied, "Oh, absolutely," and went on to cite Chaucer as an influence: "Well, I read Chaucer's *The Canterbury Tales* and that has something to do with it. But I think Faulkner has influenced me more than any other writer and, of course, *As I Lay Dying* has influenced me" (Ingram and Steinberg, 341).

18. Raboteau, 243. For another perceptive analysis of the spirituals, see W. E. B. Du Bois's "Of the Sorrow Songs" in *The Souls of Black Folk*. Two studies that trace the role of other musical forms in black American history and expression are Amiri Baraka's *Blues People: Negro Music in White America* (New York: Morrow, 1963) and Robert Palmer's *Deep Blues: A Musical and Cultural History of the Mississippi Delta* (New York: Penguin, 1981).

Chapter Three

1. Both Cable and Chopin draw on Louisiana for their literary inspiration. Cable's *The Grandissimes* (New York: Penguin, 1988), *Old Creole Days* (1879), and his more critically acclaimed *Madame Delphine* (1881) are all intimate portraits of antebellum Louisiana. Chopin's first novel, *At Fault* (New York: Green Street Press, 1986), and her two collections of short stories, *Bayou Folk* (1894) and *A Night in Acadie* (1897), use Creole manners as the core of their subjects.

2. In "'This Louisiana Thing That Drives Me'" Gaines elaborates on rural Louisiana as an inspiration in his writing. He says of the land, "I come back not as an objective observer, but as someone who must come back in order to write about Louisiana. I must come back to be with the land in different seasons, to travel the land, to go into the fields. . . . I come back to absorb things" (39).

3. For a complete history of the Acadians, see Carl Brasseaux, *The Founding of the New Acadia* (Baton Rouge: Louisiana State University Press, 1987), particularly 1–71.

4. The origin of the word *Cajun* is nebulous, but Brasseaux gives the following history: "Louisiana historians have generally failed to recognize the significant sociocultural differences existing among the state's various Francophone groups. As a result, French speakers in proximity to the Acadian settlements—even those traditionally hostile to the exiles' descendants—have been lumped together with genuine Acadians under the euphemistic label, *Cajun*" (90).

5. *Catherine Carmier* (San Francisco: Northpoint Press, 1981), 106; hereafter cited in text as *CC*.

6. For a thorough discussion of the history and social politics that influence Creoles of color, see Virginia R. Dominguez, *White by Definition: Social Classification in Creole Louisiana* (New Brunswick, N.J.: Rutgers University Press, 1986), and Gary B. Mills, *The Forgotten People: Cane River's Creoles of Color* (Baton Rouge: Louisiana State University Press, 1977). For a strong indication of the complexity inherent in the term *Creole* and the tenacious attempt of French and Spanish Creoles to divorce themselves from any hint of black heritage or relation to the Creoles of color, see M. Herrin, *The Creole Aristocracy,* (New York: Exposition Press, 1952).

7. Dominguez, *White by Definition,* 161.

8. Ruth Laney, "A Conversation with Ernest Gaines," *Southern Review* 10 (January 1974), 5–6; hereafter cited in text.

9. Madame Bayonne's naming is significant. Bayonne is the fictional setting linking all Gaines's works, and within this novel the character named after this city acts as a cohesive element as well. Her knowledge of past and present and her analytical abilities allow her to create a perspective for Jackson, one that links many disparate elements of race, ethnicity, class, and communal history.

10. Mark's fate at the hands of Raoul was indeed a tragic manifestation of a desire to eradicate the memory of an unfaithful wife, but it was also an attempt to eradicate the "taint" of blackness. Again Dominguez's work is helpful in understanding both the attitudes many Creoles of color have toward other blacks and how these attitudes affect familial relationships. She relates a less tragic and far more frequent attempt to erase evidence of African-American lineage: "Colored Creoles strive for *whitening*. . . . [T]hese Creoles impose a value hierarchy on the continuum of physical appearance; the whiter a person is, the better his status, and the blacker he is, the lower his ascribed status. Not uncommon is the case of a child

sent to the country to be raised by a grandmother or an aunt away from home, because he is too dark for the family" (162).

    11. Harold E. Toliver, "Marvell's Pastoral Vision," in *Pastoral and Romance: Modern Essays in Criticism,* ed. Eleanor Terry Lincoln (Englewood Cliffs, N.J.: Prentice Hall, 1969), 139.

    12. Erwin Panofsky gives a history of the phrase *Et in Arcadia ego* and offers a convincing argument for the correct translation as being "Death is even in Arcadia": "The correct translation of the phrase in its orthodox form is . . . not 'I, too, was born, or lived, in Arcady,' but: 'Even in Arcady there am I,' from which we must conclude that the speaker is not a deceased Arcadian shepherd or shepherdess but Death in person" (*"Et in Arcadia Ego,"* in *Pastoral and Romance,* 35). Panofsky continues, "The phrase . . . can . . . be understood to be voiced by Death personified, and can still be translated as 'Even in Arcady I, Death, hold sway'" (39).

Chapter Four

    1. In speaking of the relationship of the Lightnin' Hopkins blues song to his novel, Gaines states, "One day I was sitting around listening to a record by Lightnin' Hopkins, and these words stuck in my mind: 'The worse thing this black man ever done—when he moved his wife and family to Mr. Tim Moore's Farm. Mr. Tim Moore's man don't stand and grin; say "If you stay out the graveyard nigger, I'll keep you out the pen."' These words haunted me for weeks, for months—without my knowing why, or what I would ever do with them. . . . It took about a year . . . before it all jelled in my mind, and then I started writing, in the summer of 1968, the novel *Of Love and Dust*" ("MJ and I," 33).

    2. In *Greek Tragedy* Albin Lesky outlines the basic characteristics of tragedy as the following: (a) the presence of a hero who "appears against the somber background of inevitable death"; (b) a hero's fall from an "illusory world of security . . . into the depth of inescapable anguish"; (c) relevancy *"to the world we live in.* The fall must affect us, it should come close to us, change us"; (d) a "conflict from which there is no escape"; (e) "individual action bound up with the destiny of others—friends, comrades in arms, whole nations"; and (f) "the fate of the individual . . . seen as part of a dramatic sequence which leads inevitably to tragic events" ([New York: Barnes & Noble, 1967], 1–11; hereafter cited in text). These criteria are helpful in seeing why *Of Love and Dust* is essentially a tragedy, for all these characteristics are present in the novel: Marcus is the tragic hero; he falls from the security of his secret dealings with the landowner Hebert to the anguish of fighting the overseer Bonbon; the novel is timeless in its treatment of racial tension; and Marcus's actions affect his entire community by setting in motion a tragic sequence of events.

    3. *Of Love and Dust* (New York: W. W. Norton, 1979), 26; hereafter cited in text as *LD.*

    4. John Edgar Wideman, *"Of Love and Dust*: A Reconsideration," *Callaloo* 1, no. 3 (May 1978): 78.

5. Though Gaines does not make specific reference to Faulkner in the context of this particular work, perhaps another likeness to Faulkner can be found in the similarity of Gaines's use of Jim and Faulkner's use of choral characters, his black female characters, in particular. Dilsey in *The Sound and the Fury* might be a very familiar example. It is evident that Faulkner allows their voices to give pertinent historical, social, moral, and emotional information for understanding his characters' psychological motivations. In *Of Love and Dust* Jim functions in a similar manner.

6. In an interview, Gaines himself notes the strong similarity the Louisiana society that acts as the setting for his fiction bears to the plantation era of slavery: "By the '30s, when I was born, conditions were not too much different from the times of slavery. We were attached to the place. . . . You couldn't move around and do whatever you wanted to do. During the time I grew up, I understood much of what has been written in books about slavery and the reconstruction period, farm life and plantation life" (Steve Culpepper and Mary Broussard, "Writer Draws on Pointe Coupee Childhood, *Sunday Advocate*, 4 December 1988, 10A).

Chapter Five

1. *The Autobiography of Miss Jane Pittman* (New York: Dial Press, 1971), vii–viii; hereafter cited in text as *MJP.*

2. Interview, Tines Kendricks, *Lay My Burden Down: A Folk History of Slavery* (Chicago: University of Chicago Press, 1945), 74.

3. Charles Nichols, *Many Thousand Gone* (Bloomington: Indiana University Press, 1963), ix; hereafter cited in text.

4. For a thorough discussion of the characteristics of oral narrative, see Walter J. Ong, S.J., *Orality and Literacy: The Technologizing of the Word,* New Accents Series, ed. Terence Hawkes (New York: Methuen, 1982), 36–57.

5. Jane's description of the slaves changing names is one of many realistic chords struck throughout the work. This act occurs in many memoirs of emancipation, such as Booker T. Washington's *Up from Slavery* (New York: Penguin, 1986). It is interesting to note the parallels that exist between Jane's description of emancipation and Reconstruction, in particular the slaves' attitudes toward renaming and flight, and that of Washington. This scene is also reminiscent of one slave's recollection in *Lay My Burden Down.* In this collection of remembrances, Lee Guidon states the following: "After freedom a heap of people say they was going to name theirselves over. They named theirselves big names. . . . Some of the names was Abraham, and some called theirselves Lincum. Any big name 'cepting their master's name" (66).

6. The hunter extends Gaines's theme of sons seeking fathers to this work. When Jane asks about his family history and queries, "Your mama dead?" he responds, "No, my mama ain't dead. . . . I know where she at. . . . I want find him now" (*MJP,* 44).

7. This segment of Jane's autobiography calls to mind a work that simi-

larly details the "slavery" of sharecropping, *All God's Dangers*. In *All God's Dangers*, Nate Shaw, the fictitious name of Ned Cobb, dictates his life story to an amanuensis. He outlines his experiences as a sharecropper and the subsequent political and economic strategies he employed to free himself from a system of perpetual debt (Theodore Rosengarten, *All God's Dangers* [New York: Avon, 1974]). The continual setbacks Cobb dictates in his autobiography are also faced by Joe Pittman, as the plantation owner, Colonel Dye, fabricates obstructions to Joe's leaving.

8. Philip Durham and Everett L. Jones, *The Negro Cowboy* (New York: Dodd, Mead, 1965), 44; hereafter cited in text.

9. Gaines's own experience illustrates the difficulty of black education in rural Louisiana: "I went to school in a church. We didn't have a school. You would sit on benches or pews and your desk was your lap. . . . Or you turned around and got down on your knees and used your pew as your desk. . . . On Sundays, it was a church. Five days during the week, it was a school. The (white public school) superintendent, once or twice a year, would come by and talk for a few minutes and leave. That's probably all the visits we ever got from public school authorities. . . . We were supposed to have six months of school, but of course we didn't. You were lucky if you had five months. School didn't start until late October and you were out in early April. . . . We had [to grow] cotton until the first of October. Then, by middle of April, we began to plant and harvest other things, potatoes and whatever you had in the field. And children whose fathers were sharecroppers had to go into the fields" (Culpepper and Broussard, 10A).

10. An example of divergent philosophies of black improvement can be found through a comparison of Booker T. Washington's *Up from Slavery* and W.E.B. Du Bois's *The Souls of Black Folk* (New York: Signet, New American Library, 1969), particularly Du Bois's chapter entitled "Of Mr. Booker T. Washington and Others."

11. Marie Laveau was the legendary voodoo practitioner of New Orleans who appears in many pieces of black literature. Of her influence Raboteau gives the following account: "The voodoo cult in New Orleans came under the sway of a succession of strong leaders who traded their power of magic for profit and prestige. By means of charms, amulets, and potions they claimed to predict the future and manipulate the present. Under the strong leadership of priestesses such as Sainte Dede and especially the two Marie Laveaus, mother and daughter, voodoo enjoyed a great deal of influence among the black and white citizens of New Orleans throughout most of the nineteenth century. The long reign of the two Maries stretched from 1830 to the 1880s and included a system of domestic spies among the servant class to keep Marie informed of important secrets" (79).

12. John Callahan gives a witty and insightful interpretation of Jane's coinage of the word *retrick* and illuminates the power of language to create the illusion of change but not the reality. In his article "Image-Making: Tradition and the Two Versions of *The Autobiography of Miss Jane Pittman*," he states, "In her view . . .

retrick betrays (tricks or manipulates) the . . . people" (*Chicago Review* 29, no. 2 (Autumn, 1977), 54.

Chapter Six

1. C. Eric Lincoln, in his comprehensive history of the Black Muslims, elaborates on the Black Muslim system of naming: "To commemorate his rebirth, the convert drops his last name and is known simply by his first name and the letter X. . . . The symbol X has a double meaning: implying 'ex,' it signifies that the Muslim is no longer what he was; and as 'X,' it signifies the unknown quality or quantity. It at once repudiates the white man's name and announces the rebirth of the Black Man, endowed with a set of qualities the white man does not know" (*The Black Muslims in America* [Boston: Beacon Press, 1961], 110–11).

2. The allusion to Malcolm X through the naming of Robert provides a context for understanding the impatience of younger civil rights advocates in Phillip's community and their fear of white participation in movements for black equality. Though Gaines never makes the extreme statements Malcolm X does, Malcolm's expressed fear of the dilution of black influence portended by white participation in the civil rights movement lends insight into Gaines's work. In referring to the March on Washington as the "Farce on Washington," Malcolm X states the following: "The original 'angry' March on Washington was now about to be entirely changed. . . . Invited next to join the March were four famous white public figures: one Catholic, one Jew, one Protestant, and one labor boss. . . . It had become an outing, a picnic. . . . What originally was planned to be an angry riptide, one English newspaper aptly described now as 'the gentle flood.'. . . Talk about 'integrated'! It was like salt and pepper. . . . I observed that circus. Who ever heard of angry revolutionists all harmonizing 'We Shall Overcome . . . Suum Day . . .' while tripping and swaying along arm-in-arm with the very people they were supposed to be angrily revolting against? Who ever heard of angry revolutionists swinging their bare feet together with their oppressor in lily pad park pools, with gospels and guitars and 'I Have A Dream' speeches? . . . What that March on Washington did do was lull Negroes for a while. But inevitably, the black masses started realizing they had been smoothly hoaxed again by the white man" (*The Autobiography of Malcolm X* [New York: Grove Press, 1966], 279–81).

3. Gaines, *In My Father's House* (New York: W. W. Norton, 1978), 3–4; hereafter cited in text as *FH*.

Chapter Seven

1. Richard Wright, *Native Son* (New York: Harper & Row, 1966), xiv; hereafter cited in the text.

2. None of the white authorities in *Native Son* believe Bigger to be capable of creating the elaborate alibi he does. They fault Jan for conceiving of the kidnap plot, and a newspaper item states of Mary's murder, "Police are not yet satisfied

with the account [Jan] Erlone has given of himself and are of the conviction that he may be linked to the Negro as an accomplice; they feel that the plan of the murder and kidnapping was too elaborate to be the work of a Negro mind" (229). Bigger's disappointed response after reading the account of the authorities' misconception shows how much Mary's murder has become his creative opus: "At that moment he wanted to walk out into the street and up to a policeman and say, 'No Jan didn't help me! He didn't have a damn thing to do with it! I—I did it!' His lips twisted in a smile that was half-leer and half-defiance" (229–30).

3. *A Gathering of Old Men* (New York: Vintage, Random House, 1984), 58; hereafter cited in the text as *GM*.

4. Paul Laurence Dunbar, "The Poet," *The Collected Poems of Paul Laurence Dunbar* (New York: Dodd, Mead, 1965). In this poem Dunbar expresses his frustration over the duality of consciousness imposed upon him and provides an interesting insight into the experience Gaines expresses through his character Chimley. Viewing himself as a poet, Dunbar sought recognition solely on those terms, as manifested in his desire to use standard English as the language for his poetry. Many of his readers, however, viewed him solely as a "darky" poet and demanded that he write poems in dialect, saying he was more competent in this form. In an interview with Charles Rowell, Gaines himself made an interesting comment on white perceptions of black literary artists when he stated, "I've always felt that the white man out there would rather we did not use the proper language. He would rather that all we did was scream and make noises. He would prefer that our aim was not perfection" (Rowell, 46). In a sense Gaines's observations echo Dunbar's experience of dual existence. In Chimley, Gaines fashions a symbol of the duality plaguing African Americans who are keenly aware that the humanity they share with others is denied by their society.

5. Reynolds Price, "A Louisiana Pageant of Calamity," *New York Times Book Review*, 30 October 1983, 15.

6. David Bevington, *From "Mankind" to Marlowe* (Cambridge, Mass.: Harvard University Press, 1968), 9.

7. In her description of characters of mixed blood, Stowe consistently credits their desire for freedom to their white ancestry. In describing George Harris, for example, she states, "We remark, *en passant*, that George was, by his father's side, of white descent. . . . From one of the proudest families in Kentucky he had inherited a set of fine European features, and a high, indomitable spirit" (182). This description contrasts sharply with the physical description of Uncle Tom, "a large, broad-chested, powerfully made man, of a full glossy black," and with his docility. Upon learning that another mulatto character in the work, Eliza, plans to flee slavery, Tom's comments imply that her white lineage gives her the nature and right to do so and that his full black heritage does not do the same for him: "No, no—I an't going. Let Eliza go—it's her right! I wouldn't be the one to say no—'tan't *natur* for her to stay. . . . If I must be sold, or all the people on the place, and everything go to rack, why, let me be sold. I s'pose I can b'ar it as well as any on 'em" (90). In *Clotel*,

William Wells Brown, the son of a slave woman and her master, reveals sentiments similar to Stowe's when he states, "The infusion of Anglo-Saxon with African blood has created an insurrectionary feeling among the slaves of America hitherto unknown. Aware of their blood connection with their owners, these mulattoes labour under the sense of their personal and social injuries; and tolerate, if they do not encourage in themselves, low and vindictive passions" (171). Implicit in both these texts is the assumption that it is a greater tragedy to enslave a person of biracial lineage and more in keeping with the "natural order" to enslave those of purely African descent.

Chapter Eight

    1. James Weldon Johnson, *God's Trombones* (New York: Viking Press, 1969), 8.

    2. Harriet Wilson was a free black woman whose novel argued that the indentured servitude of the North bore a striking resemblance to the slavery of the South. In addition to desiring an end to maltreatment, Wilson also had a very pragmatic reason for writing her novel: the financial support of her and her son. See *Our Nig* (New York: Random, Vintage, 1983), preface.

    3. In *Many Thousand Gone,* Charles Nichols gives a history of the nature of the creation of the slave narrative: "There is no doubt that most of the narratives were produced with the aid of the anti-slavery men of Boston and New York, and contain literary, ethical and sentimental elements added by the white ghost writers and editors. Indeed it has often been charged that most of the narratives were, in effect, written by abolitionists to whom they were sometimes dictated. . . . [A]bolitionist editorship does not necessarily impugn their reliability, for only superficial aspects of narratives have been challenged and even fictionalized accounts are striking in their essential truth. As the victim's personal account of bondage, these autobiographies provide a unique and essential perspective on American slavery" (x). In his article "The First Fifty Years of the Slave Narrative, 1760–1810," William Andrews gives this account of abolitionist assistance in the writing of narratives: "[A]manuensis-editors of early slave narratives . . . accommodate the stories of their subjects to the organizing and selection principles and the cultural values of popular white autobiographical genres, in particular, the captivity narrative, the conversion account, the criminal confession, the spiritual pilgrimage, and the journal of ministerial labors. Within the boundaries of these genres, black self-portraits were cropped and framed according to the standards of an alien culture. For the most part, then, the intention of early slave narratives was primarily to celebrate the acculturation of the black man into established categories of the white social order" (in *The Art of the Slave Narrative,* ed. John Sekora and Darwin T. Turner [Macomb: Western Illinois University Press, 1982], 8).

    4. In *The Colloquial Style in America* (New York: Oxford University Press, 1966), Richard Bridgman offers an insightful sociocultural explanation of the popularity of the dialect form within the frame stories of Harris, Nelson, and Page. As

he defines it, the frame story used standard English to quarantine the vernacular and a "literate narrator" to introduce the vernacular speaker. This scheme "permitted the reader to enjoy colorful informality, yet be assured that the hierarchy of social values still stood, that the vulgar were still under control" (23).

5. "A Survey: Black Writers' Views on Literary Lions and Values," *Negro Digest* 17 (January 1968): 13; hereafter cited in text as "LL".

6. Review of *The Autobiography of Miss Jane Pittman, New York Times Book Review,* 23 May 1971, 12.

Selected Bibliography

PRIMARY WORKS

Novels

The Autobiography of Miss Jane Pittman. New York: Dial Press, 1971.
Catherine Carmier. San Francisco: Northpoint Press, 1981.
A Gathering of Old Men. New York: Vintage, Random House, 1984.
In My Father's House. New York: W. W. Norton, 1978.
Of Love and Dust. New York: W. W. Norton, 1979.

Story Collection

Bloodline. New York: W. W. Norton, 1976.

Articles

"Miss Jane and I." *Callaloo* 1, no. 3 (May 1978): 23–38.
"Home: A Photo-Essay." *Callaloo* 1, no. 3 (May 1978): 52–67.

SECONDARY WORKS

Articles

Andrews, William L. "'We Ain't Going Back There': The Idea of Progress in *The Autobiography of Miss Jane Pittman*." *Black American Literary Forum* 11 (Winter 1977): 146–9. Asserts that Gaines paints personalized and intimate portraits of progress within the rural South, historically an unchanging region.

Aubert, Alvin. "Ernest Gaines's Truly Tragic Mulatto." *Callaloo* 1, no. 3 (May 1978): 68–75. Compares Gaines's treatment of the mulatto character with those typically found in literature.

———. "Self-Reintegration through Self-Confrontation." *Callaloo* 1, no. 3 (May 1978): 132–35. Aubert reviews *In My Father's House* and examines the confrontations that lead to the emergence of a new Phillip Martin.

Beckman, Barry. "Jane Pittman and Oral Tradition." *Callaloo* 1, no. 3 (May 1978): 102–9. A study of the influence of oral tradition in the creation of Gaines's language within *The Autobiography of Miss Jane Pittman*.

Bryant, Jerry H. "Ernest J. Gaines: Change, Growth, and History." *Southern Review* 10 (October 1984): 851–64. Analyzes the novels of Ernest Gaines, with particular attention to those major themes and elements which make him a classic southern American writer.

Byerman, Keith E. "Ernest Gaines." In *Dictionary of Literary Biography,* vol. 33, *Afro-American Writers: 1955–Present,* edited by Thadious M. Davis and Trudier Harris, 84–96. Detroit: Gale Research, 1984. A critical biography of Ernest Gaines.

Callahan, John F. "Hearing Is Believing: The Landscape of Voice in Ernest Gaines's *Bloodline.*" *Callaloo* 7, no. 1 (Winter 1984): 86–112. An investigation of the relationship between voice, history, and individual identity in Gaines's collection of short stories.

––––––. "Image-Making: Tradition and the Two Versions of *The Autobiography of Miss Jane Pittman.*" *Chicago Review* 29 no. 2 (Autumn 1977): 45–62. A mixture of personal memoir and analysis that uses a comparison of Irish-American and African-American experiences with racism to establish a context for the investigation of the differences between the novel and the television movie made from it.

Davis, Thadious M. "Headlands and Quarters: Louisiana in *Catherine Carmier.* *Callaloo* 7, no. 2 (Spring 1984): 1–13. Reviews the influence of Gaines's boyhood Louisiana landscape on his novel.

Duncan, Todd. "Scene and Life Cycle in Ernest Gaines's *Bloodline.*" *Callaloo* 1, no. 3 (May 1978): 85–101. An examination of the life-cycle motif, as outlined by Erik Erickson's eight epigenetic phases, in the short stories of Ernest Gaines.

Fabre, Michel. "Bayonne or the Yoknapatawpha of Ernest Gaines," *Callaloo* 1, no. 3 (May 1978): 110–23. Uses Faulkner's creation of Yoknapatawpha to investigate Gaines's depiction of the South and its complex racial relations in his fictitious Bayonne.

Giles, James P. "Revolution and Myth: William Melvin Kelly's *A Different Drummer* and Ernest Gaines' *The Autobiography of Miss Jane Pittman.*" *Minority Voices* 1, no. 2 (1971): 39–48. A comparison of the use of myth as a signifier for revolutionary change in the works of Kelly and Gaines.

Grant, William E. "Ernest Gaines." In *Dictionary of Literary Biography,* vol. 2, *American Novelists Since World War II,* edited by Joel Myerson, 170–75. Detroit: Gale Research, 1978. A critical biography of Ernest Gaines.

Greene, J. Lee. "The Pain and the Beauty: The South, the Black Writer, and Conventions of the Picaresque." In *The American South: Portrait of a Culture,* edited by Louis D. Rubin, Jr., 264–88. Baton Rouge: Louisiana State University Press, 1980. An analysis of the depictions of the South as a shaping influence on the main characters of James Weldon Johnson's *Autobiography of an Ex-Colored Man,* Jean Toomer's *Cane,* Ralph Ellison's *Invisible Man,* and Ernest Gaines's *The Autobiography of Miss Jane Pittman.*

Hicks, Jack. "To Make These Bones Live: History and Community in Ernest Gaines's Fiction." *Black American Literary Forum* 11 (Spring 1977): 9–19. Reviews the influence of the black folk tradition and history on Gaines's fiction.

Pettis, Joyce. "The Black Historical Novel as Best Seller." *Kentucky Folklore Record* 25 (1979): 51–59. Examines the reasons for the success of *Miss Jane*.

Roberts, John W. "The Individual and the Community in Two Short Stories by Ernest J. Gaines." *Black American Literary Forum* 18, no. 3 (Fall 1984): 110–13. Analyzes the relationship of the black individual to his or her larger cultural community.

Rowell, Charles H. "Ernest J. Gaines: A Checklist, 1964–1978." *Callaloo* 1, no. 3 (May 1978): 125–31. A concise listing of bibliographic materials, interviews, books, reviews, biographical materials, and essays on Ernest Gaines.

Shelton, Frank W. "Ambiguous Manhood in Ernest J. Gaines's *Bloodline*." *College Language Association Journal* 19 (December 1975): 200–9. Reviews the various definitions of manhood present in Gaines's short stories.

Stoelting, Winifred L. "Human Dignity and Pride in the Novels of Ernest Gaines." *College Language Association Journal* 14 (March 1971): 340–58. Examines the manner in which the characters of *Catherine Carmier* and *Of Love and Dust* maintain dignity and self-esteem against all odds.

Wideman, John Edgar. "Of Love and Dust: A Reconsideration." *Callaloo* 1, no. 3 (May 1978): 78. Through analyzing the relationship of Marcus and Louise, Wideman explores the subtlety of racial relationships, Gaines's use of myth and language, and his use of symbols and imagery throughout his entire canon.

Interviews

Beauford, Fred. "A Conversation with Ernest J. Gaines." *Black Creation* 4 (Fall 1972): 16–18. Discusses with Gaines his background, influences, and attitudes toward literary composition.

Culpepper, Steve, and **Mary Broussard.** "Writer Draws on Point Coupee Childhood." *Sunday Advocate,* 4 December 1988, 10A. In an interview, Gaines discusses his community and its influence on his fiction.

Desruisseaux, Paul. "Ernest Gaines: A Conversation." *New York Times Book Review,* 11 June 1978, 12+. An interview with Ernest Gaines upon the publication of *In My Father's House*.

Fuller, Hoyt. "Black Writers' Views on Literary Lions and Values." *Negro Digest* 17 (January 1968): 10–89. The results of a survey polling 38 black writers, among them Ernest Gaines, and asking for opinions on many topics: the role of the black writer in America, literary influences, personal aims as writers.

Gemmett, Robert, and **Philip Gerber.** "An Interview: Ernest J. Gaines." *New Orleans Review* 1 (Summer 1969): 331–35. A conversation with Ernest J.

Gaines, resulting from the Writers Forum Program at the State University of New York at Brockport.

Gross, Robert A. "The Black Novelists: 'Our Turn.'" *Newsweek,* 16 June 1969, 94[+]. A survey of the art-politics tension faced by Ernest Gaines and other black writers of the turbulent sixties.

Ingram, Forrest, and Barbara Steinberg. "On the Verge: An Interview with Ernest J. Gaines." *New Orleans Review* 3 (1972): 339–44. An interview concentrating on Gaines's more recent works, *The Autobiography of Miss Jane Pittman* and *In My Father's House.*

Laney, Ruth. "A Conversation with Ernest Gaines." *Southern Review* 10 (January 1974): 1–14. An interview with Ernest Gaines in which he reveals the importance of his background and the oral tradition to his works.

Rowell, Charles H. "'This Louisiana Thing That Drives Me': An Interview with Ernest J. Gaines." *Callaloo* 1, no. 3 (May 1978): 39–51. An interview with Gaines that reveals the importance of Louisiana environment, history, myth, and language forms in the creation of his fiction.

Reviews

Blackburn, Sara. Review of *Of Love and Dust,* by Ernest J. Gaines. *Bergen [New Jersey] Record,* 24 April 1977, B4.

Granat, Robert. "Loner on Olympus." *New York Times,* 19 November 1967, 83. A Review of *Of Love and Dust.*

Lafore Laurence. "Various Vehicles." *New York Times Book Review,* 29 September 1968. A comparative review of three collections of short stories: Harry Brewster's *Into Deeper Waters,* David Ely's *Time Out,* and Ernest Gaines's *Bloodline.*

Price, Reynolds. "A Louisiana Pageant of Calamity." *New York Times Book Review,* 30 October 1983, 15. A review of *A Gathering of Old Men.*

Review of *Catherine Carmier. New York Times Literary Supplement,* 10 February 1966, 97.

Review of *Of Love and Dust. New York Times Literary Supplement,* 1 August 1967, D17.

Review of *Bloodline. New York Times Book Review,* 29 September 1968, 73.

Review of *The Autobiography of Miss Jane Pittman. New York Times Book Review,* 10 August 1975, 23.

Review of *In My Father's House. New York Times Book Review,* 11 June 1978, 13.

Walker, Alice. "The Autobiography of Miss Jane Pittman." *New York Times Book Review,* 23 May 1971, 6[+].

Watkins, Mel. "Books of the Times." *New York Times,* 20 July 1978, 13. Review of *In My Father's House.*

GENERAL BACKGROUND INFORMATION

Books on Black History and Culture

Baraka, Amiri. *Blues People: Negro Music in White America and the Music That Developed from It.* New York: Morrow, 1963. Baraka places jazz and blues within the context of American and African-American social history. Music becomes a metaphor for cultural, economic, and spiritual history. The work assists in understanding the importance of musical forms, particularly the rural blues, to Gaines's themes.

Botkin, B. A., ed. *Lay My Burden Down: A Folk History of Slavery.* Chicago: University of Chicago Press, 1945. Former slaves' reminiscences of bondage, emancipation, and day-to-day life in a compilation of selected narratives gathered under the Federal Writers Project.

Childs, John Brown. *The Political Black Minister: A Study in Afro-American Politics and Religion.* Boston: G. K. Hall, 1980. A history of black political action within the church and a case study of three black ministers who balance spiritual and political leadership. The work is helpful as a background for understanding Gaines's depoliticization of his black ministers.

Dominguez, Virginia R. *White by Definition: Social Classification in Creole Louisiana.* New Brunswick, N.J.: Rutgers University Press, 1986. A history of Creole Louisiana and an anthropological investigation into the complex definition of race among the Creole communities. Provides a good historical complement for Gaines's treatment of Creoles.

Du Bois, W. E. B. *The Souls of Black Folk.* New York: New American Library, Signet, 1969. A classic collection of essays analyzing the essence and position of black Americans in the United States. Particularly helpful in understanding Gaines's use of religion and religious figures.

Durham, Philip, and **Everett L. Jones.** *The Negro Cowboys.* New York: Dodd, Mead, 1965. A history of African-Americans in frontier settlements and their subsequent absence in the history and folklore of the West. A good complement for understanding the history that is part of Joe Pittman's story.

Genovese, Eugene. *Roll Jordan Roll: The World The Slaves Made.* New York: Pantheon/Random, 1974. A history of slavery in the United States and a discussion of its legacy. Helpful in understanding Gaines's crafting of historical personages, such as the slave minister.

Herskovits, Melville J. *The Myth of the Negro Past.* Boston: Beacon Press, 1958. An investigation of the African past that gave rise to black culture and of the atavisms of African culture to be found in modern African-American culture. A good resource for further information on hoodoo and conjure.

Johnson, James Weldon. *God's Trombones.* New York: Viking Press, 1969. A collection of Johnson's poetry. Contains a valuable introduction discussing the problems of defining a black aesthetic.

Lincoln, Charles Eric. *The Black Muslims in America.* Boston: Beacon Press, 1961. A comprehensive analysis of Elijah Muhammad and the Black Muslims, their history, philosophy, and impact in the United States. A work that assists in analyzing the milieu, construction, and impact of Gaines's revolutionary characters.

Nichols, Charles. *Many Thousand Gone: The Ex-Slaves' Account of Their Bondage and Freedom.* Bloomington: Indiana University Press, 1963. In this exhaustive study, Nichols gathers narratives that reveal the psychological experience of slavery from the slave's perspective. The work provides a context for understanding the central role of perspective in *Miss Jane.*

Palmer, Robert. *Deep Blues: A Musical and Cultural History of the Mississippi Delta.* New York: Penguin, 1981. Palmer cites blues as the cornerstone of American popular music, and by chronicling the life of its great personages, chronicles the history of blues from its rural roots to its migration to urban centers. Reveals why the blues are such a significant literary influence in African-American writings.

Raboteau, Albert J. *Slave Religion: The "Invisible Institution" in the Antebellum South.* New York: Oxford University Press, 1978. A history of black religious organization in slavery and after. Very helpful in understanding Gaines's use of hoodoo and his symbolic use of spiritual leaders.

Wright, Richard. *Native Son.* New York: Harper & Row, 1966. A realistic portrayal of the life of Bigger Thomas and the determinism rooted in the racism and poverty that govern him. The frustration and impotency Bigger seeks to exorcise are similar to those of Gaines's black men, young and old.

Books on Louisiana History and Culture

Brasseaux, Carl A. *The Founding of New Acadia: The Beginnings of Acadian Life in Louisiana 1765–1803.* Baton Rouge: Louisiana State University Press, 1987. A history of the Cajuns who migrated from Nova Scotia to Louisiana, as well as a compilation of social life and customs among modern Cajuns. Helpful to understanding the relationship between African Americans and Cajuns in Gaines's fiction.

Esman, Marjorie. *Henderson Louisiana: Cultural Adaptation in a Cajun Community.* New York: Holt, Rinehart & Winston, 1985. A contemporary anthropological case study of the tourist trade, customs, cooking, and racial attitudes of the Cajun residents of Henderson, Louisiana. Helpful in understanding the characterization of Gaines's Cajun characters.

Herrin, M. *The Creole Aristocracy.* New York: Exposition Press, 1952. A history designed to distinguish between Creoles of color and Creoles of Spanish and French descent, and to familiarize readers with prominent members of the Creole class. The work is somewhat dated, but it gives valuable insight into the complex distinctions involved in the Creole history of New Orleans.

Mills, Gary. *The Forgotten People, Cane River's Creoles of Color.* Baton Rouge:

Louisiana State University Press, 1977. A history of the Metoyers, who are considered a distinct racial group and who formed their own community along the Cane River. The work provides insight into the social codes that govern the beliefs and actions of Gaines's Creoles of color.

Books on General American History and Culture

Bridgman, Richard. *The Colloquial Style in America.* New York: Oxford University Press, 1966. Bridgman discusses the racial, social, and class implications of the various nonstandard literary language forms found in nineteenth-century American literature. Very useful in understanding the complexity of evolving a black aesthetic and in creating a context for understanding Gaines's remarkable use of language.

Brodie, Fawn. *Thomas Jefferson: An Intimate History.* New York: W. W. Norton, 1974. An illuminating and exhaustive biography of Jefferson, drawing upon previously neglected sources. A good companion for understanding the significance of the tragic mulatto figure in Gaines's literature.

Index

The Author

Valerie Babb received her B.A. from Queens College of the City University of New York in 1977 and her M.A. and Ph.D. in English from the State University of New York at Buffalo in 1981. She is currently assistant professor of English at Georgetown University. Her Ph.D. dissertation, "The Evolution of an American Literary Language," investigated the cultural implications of particular language forms. The presence of the oral tradition and its progeny in African American literature continues to be the focus of her research interests: within this area she has published articles on Charles Chesnutt, Zora Neale Hurston, and Alice Walker.

The Editor

Frank Day is a professor of English at Clemson University. He is the author of *Sir William Empson: An Annotated Bibliography* and *Arthur Koestler: A Guide to Research*. He was a Fulbright lecturer in American Literature in Romania (1980–81) and in Bangladesh (1986–87).